MODELING
SUCCESS

Praise for
MODELING SUCCESS

⌐ CLIENTS

"Suzanne Von Schaack is the real deal. An accomplished model, actress and producer with an impeccable reputation. She is a loving friend and an inspiration to all that know her. Suzanne shares her extensive knowledge and insight into the world of modeling, offering an honest, kind and transparent viewpoint delivered in a fun and generous manner. This book is a must have!"

~ Crista Klayman, Director of Runway L.A. Models Inc.

"Suzanne has been a dedicated career professional in the modeling and entertainment industry for many years. If there is anyone who can answer your questions and has all the answers ... it's Suzanne."

~ Joey Hunter, Consultant for the Fashion and Entertainment Industry

"I've had the pleasure to know and work with Suzanne for ten years now. Not only have we created an amazing work relationship, we've developed an extremely valued and close friendship. Over the years, we've collaborated on over 20 fashion shows and events where she hired our models to work her second to none events. We've also been honored to sign some of the top models in the world that she personally discovered and trained. When one thinks of Suzanne, five things come to mind: attention to detail, drive, creativity, class and integrity. These attributes set her apart from others in the industry and make her one of the top fashion show coordinators, model trainers and managers around. I've really appreciated having Suzanne as a colleague over these years, value our friendship, and the synergy we've developed is unequaled."

~ William Scott Whitfield, Luft Agency

"It's easy for most to go through life thinking they are hard workers, until they've met Suzanne. As one of the most self-driven humans you'll ever meet, Suzanne strives for flawlessness in all she does; it's a rare quality to find in models, especially these days. Yet Suzanne's accomplishments speak for themselves, working with the top modeling agencies in the world, curating countless fashion shows, coaching up-and-coming models and raising a family. It's no wonder she continues to be a positive influence on so many, including myself. I am truly grateful to call her a friend. May Suzanne's work continue to serve as a reminder, how glorious it is to be daring, to be caring, and to follow your dreams no matter how big they may seem."

~ Ronald Patterson, Past President of JRP / Founder of iPOP!

"Suzanne has been a business associate for over 20 years. In that time, she has created some of the most incredible fashion shows that continually wow audiences from across the globe year after year. She has a great gift of working with new talent, building their confidence, and turning them into runway stars in the matter of a few days. She has worked with most of iPOP!'s famous runway models and helped skyrocket their careers. Her eye for attention to detail is as astonishing as her creative expression. She is a consummate professional, and a joyous person to know. Thank you!"

~ Kirsten Poulin, President iPOP!

"When I think of absolute beauty and grace along with an amazing sense of style and production expertise, one name comes to mind. That is Suzanne Von Schaack. Vistas for Children has been in the capable hands of Suzanne for several years with each year being even better than the last. Suzanne and her team don't miss a step, and the level of professionalism shines through all they do. Thank you, Suzanne, for helping us put on a first-class fashion show experience for our guests. Because of your work, we have been able to raise millions of dollars for children with special needs."

~ Teri Nelson Carpenter, Past President of Vistas for Children

"I had the rewarding opportunity to work closely with Suzanne and her team on a video and photo shoot for our skincare brand, Clarisma. I was truly impressed with her depth of knowledge on modeling, photography, and video production. Her direction was clear and concise, and always remained on point. Suzanne's ability to effectively communicate to the models, photographer, and videographer was impressive. She is exemplary at many things and excels at visualizing a project and seeing it through. Without her clear direction and vision, the project would have taken much longer to complete. We are thrilled with both the outstanding results and her excellent work. Our video was used to gain distribution in Ulta Beauty. Her professionalism, knowledge and ability to instruct and inspire on camera is truly an inspiration."

~ Ameann DeJohn, Co-Founder Clarisma Beauty

"I first worked with Suzanne many years ago when she modeled for one of our fashion shows. She was the most professional person on and off the stage. Since then, we have been fortunate to have worked with Suzanne as our producer on many events over the years to highlight our members' fashion lines. For the past six years, Suzanne has taken charge of our annual fundraiser held at the historic Union Station. We are so very fortunate to have her part of our team. Not only is she professional, but she is also great to work with and totally understands the mission of our shows that draws around a thousand attendees."

~ Frances Harder, Founder and President of Fashion for Profit

"I have worked with Suzanne for many years and she is extremely talented and an expert at what she does. She has an amazing ability to synchronize music and movement to produce an absolutely beautiful show. Her unique vision and insight to cast the right people in the right places empowers the models and brings the very best out of them. We have benefited from her expertise for years and are so thankful for the many successful shows she has given us."

~ Colleen Pace, Moderator Holy Cross Mother's Guild Notre Dame High School

⬧ STUDENTS / PARENTS

"Transformation from a lanky, self-effacing girl to a poised, and dare I say, classy young woman! Suzanne introduced me to a life I had only seen in movies or magazines. She taught me accountability, when I would show up to a runway class late or had forgotten proper shoes. She also taught me professionalism. Beginning at 16, I learned how to converse with agents and connect with new clients. Suzanne dedicated her personal time to me as well, deepening our relationship from coach and student, to caring mentor. She even invited me into her home to discuss my progress with agencies or castings. Ultimately, she introduced me to my first agent. She would sit with me in her kitchen and go over dozens of photos from a photo shoot making sure I was ready to meet agencies in New York. She booked appointments for me there and in Los Angeles to help springboard my career. And she taught me to respect myself. When I look back to these moments I spent with Suzanne, I realize that I wasn't as appreciative of all her efforts. I didn't grasp how much time she was taking out of her own life because she saw promise in me. Suzanne's influence has directly impacted me as a young woman. I am now 21 years old, studying psychology in Austria and I am still modeling. Suzanne has watched my metamorphosis over the span of five years becoming the person I am today. I learned how to approach life without fear and to keep trying even when all else seems to fail. This amazing woman encouraged me to travel and study with applying my skills. For all of these reasons, I am forever in her debt and grateful."

~ *Chloe Zhorne / 21 years old*

"My daughter Chloe has had a nearly transformational experience under the wisdom and insight of Suzanne Von Schaack. We knew absolutely nothing about the modeling world until Suzanne, in her own step-by-step way shared not only her professionalism and knowledge, but also her personal touch and gentle encouragements. Suzanne seems to know everyone in the business and made those critical connections for my daughter Chloe. She made arrangements for her to audition for LA Fashion Week and introduced Chloe to her first agent. Suzanne went out of her way to arrange special trainings so my daughter could work on finer points. During those times I was mesmerized by how Suzanne got her to make huge strides with just a word or two. Throughout this entire process, my daughter's confidence has blossomed to the amazing young woman she has become. I would like to thank Suzanne for her nearly parental offerings in this way. Blessings!"

~ *Jeff Zhorne, Chloe's dad*

"Suzanne is a wonderful person and has been a fantastic mentor for my modeling career. She put me in contact with so many important people within the modeling industry and offers incredible support. I am always able to go to her with questions or if I need help with something. Suzanne always knows the right thing to say and do. Her attention to detail in terms of coaching and advice has helped me with all aspects of the business and has given me the confidence I need to advance in my career. She also placed me with my agent."

~ *Olivia Polite, 18 / Los Angeles*

"Suzanne has been an amazing resource for everything related to starting a modeling career. I trust her advice and guidance and know she has my daughter's best interests at heart. Her experience as a model and a fashion show producer makes her an invaluable resource, and she is always so generous and kind with her time and knowledge. I will always be grateful to Suzanne for everything she has done for my daughter as she embarks on this journey."

~ *Lynn Polite, Olivia's mom*

"My experience with Miss Suzanne has been amazing. When I have a question, she is very encouraging and helpful. I always look forward to our online class because we always have a good time and I learn so much. I am new to the modeling industry, but Miss Suzanne helped me gain confidence, making me a better model. She has given me so much advice. Because of her knowledge, I know how to present myself and prepare for an audition. I am so thankful to you Miss Suzanne! I really appreciate you so much."

~ Breanna Beech, 11 years old

"My experience as a parent with Suzanne Von Schaack is comforting. I don't feel that I have to be right next to my daughter while they work together in the online modeling class. Suzanne is gentle, calm, encouraging and just awesome at what she does. When she critiques my daughter, she works harder and it makes her better. We are new to the modeling business. Breanna is doing great because of Miss Suzanne. We can't thank you enough. Miss Suzanne, my daughter and I just love you!"

~ Alona Beech, Breanna's Mom

"I have been working with Suzanne Von Schaack since 2018. Having the opportunity to work with her and getting to know Suzanne will always be one on my favorite parts of my modeling career journey. She taught me how to turn my pageant walk into a runway walk. She taught me the difference between modeling for high fashion versus commercial work. She also taught me how to carry myself and how to navigate in this industry. Without having the chance to work with Suzanne, I know for a fact that my modeling career wouldn't be half of what it is right now. I think I would still be the shy girl with a pipe dream that didn't know how to act in front of a camera. I owe my present and future success to Suzanne because she has always supported me and believed in me. No one has done even a fraction of what Suzanne is still doing for me to advance my career. Suzanne helped make my dreams come true!"

~ Alyssa Finney

"It was an honor to meet Suzanne Von Schaack in California where my son was an amateur model. After working with Miss Suzanne, we knew her heart was made of gold. When the opportunity came back around to do one-on-one training with her online, we were all elated. We knew her passion and knowledge for the industry would ensure our son would receive the best training. Chance is an aspiring model with the desire to learn and grow. After the first training with her, he had the desire and the confidence to practice on his own. Each class was full of knowledge. Miss Suzanne's training covered every aspect of the business, such as runway modeling, commercial print, diet and exercise, as well as information regarding great hygiene. We see the growth, passion and confidence in Chance because she provided a solid foundation for him to stand on. Thank you, Miss Suzanne forever!"

~ Monicia Rogers, Chance's mom

"Thank you, Suzanne, for making Caterina part of such an impressive show! We've spent some time on your website and after viewing all of your accomplishments and recognition, we are even more proud to be able to say that Caterina had the privilege of working with you. We would be honored to have her be a part of one of your future projects. In fact, Caterina has not stopped talking about you and the girls she met during the showcase. Thank you!"

~ Cindy Teufel, Caterina's mom

"Suzanne's modeling course helps kids develop their inner self, personality and discover more of themselves. I believe that modeling class is for everybody. It doesn't matter if you want to be a model, actor, singer, dancer or just be a kid. This class is a must! Suzanne, thank you for your time, sharing your techniques and your patience."

~ Mary, mom

MODELING SUCCESS

YOU HAVE THE QUESTION. I HAVE THE ANSWER.

SUZANNE VON SCHAACK

SUZANNE VON SCHAACK
PRODUCTIONS

Suzanne Von Schaack Productions
www.SuzanneVonSchaack.com

Limits of Liability and Disclaimer of Warranty.
The author and publisher shall not be liable for your misuse of this material. This book is strictly for informational and educational purposes.

Warning – Disclaimer.
The purpose of this book is to educate and entertain. The author and/or publisher do not guarantee that anyone following these techniques, suggestions, tips, ideas, or strategies will become successful. The author and/or publisher shall have neither liability nor responsibility to anyone with respect to any loss or damage caused, or alleged to be caused, directly or indirectly by the information contained in this book.

ISBN 978-0-578-82973-9 paperback
Library of Congress Cataloging-in-Publishing Data is available upon request.

Printed in the United States of America
First Printing, 2021

Creative Direction and Editing by Susie Augustin www.GetBrandedPress.com
Cover & Interior Design by Kateryna Korniienko-Heidtman
Cover Photography by many photographers, including Danika Singfield,
Rodolphe Haussaire, L'Official Magazine
Back Cover Photography by Michael Hiller
Business Card design by Paula Saunders, Fashion Fix

Dedication

I dedicate this book to all of you who share
the same dream that I had as a young girl...
To become a model.

This book is packed with information to inform you
and to guide you along your journey to make your
Dreams Come True.

Acknowledgments

With over 40 years of experience in the modeling industry, it is with sheer joy and excitement that I present my book, *Modeling Success*. I have had an exciting and lucrative career as a model during the 70s, 80s and 90s in NYC, Los Angeles, Paris and Milan. I am in gratitude to all of the agents who have represented me over the years and to the many clients who have booked me.

Currently, I produce, create and direct large fashion show events in Los Angeles and Las Vegas. I also produce and procure video docs for website use to help companies brand and promote their product lines. Through this genre of work, I met Ameann DeJohn. Ameann and I share a love for creativity which promoted growth and respect to help each of us in our endeavors. I respectively thank Ameann for introducing me to Susie Augustin. With Susie's guidance, encouragement, friendship and knowledge, she made the writing of my book simple and easy. Susie knows her craft and generously guided me through this journey.

Robert Amico, my friend and confidant, challenged me to write, produce and star in my own short film *The Chains That Bind*. Because of what Robert saw in me that I did not see in myself, I took on that challenge. That short film had great success at film festivals winning many prestigious awards. With that success behind me, I was able to challenge myself to write this book.

To the most important people in my life, my family. Danielle, Cary, Carson and Weston McCall, you give me so much love, encouragement and support in everything that I do. You breathe life into me and through me. It is with the greatest of gratitude that I acknowledge and dedicate this book to you, my family.

Table Of Contents

Introduction

So many of us grow up having dreams that seem beyond our reach. I am one of those people. I lived in a small farm town in the Midwest. I loved this quaint, simple town Darlington, Wisconsin, where I grew up. I'm not sure if those who grew up in that town of 2,000 people had the same lofty ideas and dreams that I had, but I knew I wanted to one day move away to see the world and discover new things.

I was very tall as a young girl. I was teased and called "Giraffe" because I was so much taller than everyone in my class. Other people would tell me that I should be a model. One day I stumbled upon an advertisement in the newspaper regarding model training in Madison, Wisconsin. It was there that my dream began taking its first flight.

I eventually made it to NYC to be in a modeling competition. After that competition, I stayed in NYC. It was then that the hard work began. It wasn't easy for me in the beginning. It took time for me to get my career off the ground. But I did it! I worked with some of the best photographers and designers in the business. In NYC, I was represented by Wilhelmina Agency and later the Ford Agency. For runway, I was represented by Mannequin Agency and Foster Fell Agency. I also had agents in Milan (Ricardo Guy Agency) and in Paris (Glamour Agency).

After living and working in NYC for 14 years, I moved to California. I continued my modeling career in Los Angeles, where I pursued acting as well. I have booked several roles as an actor, but I am most known for my modeling career. I am also known for producing charity fashion shows.

When I look back at my career as a model, I can't help but think that had I met the right mentor to guide me in my journey, I could have moved my career along much more quickly. When I meet young people who have the dream and the potential to be a model, I offer them the mentorship I wish I would have had in my own career. I coach them in private or online classes and introduce them to agents to help them obtain representation. However, I found myself asking, "What about those young people who live in rural areas like I did, who don't have any idea where to begin or how to make their dreams come true?" As a result, I decided to write this book, hoping that it would reach everyone everywhere. I have put all of my knowledge and expertise into this book for all of you who share the dream to become a model. This book is for those who live near or far. It's for those that live in a big city or perhaps in a small, quaint, simple farm town in the Midwest, like where I grew up and **dared to dream.**

CHAPTER 1

DIFFERENT TYPES OF MODELING

What are the different types of modeling?

There are many types of modeling. Print and Runway are the focus of the modeling business. In this chapter, I break it all down for you to have a clear understanding of each category.

RUNWAY MODELING

A runway model has very specific qualifications in height, size, measurements and attitude. They must also know how to walk the catwalk, aka the runway. A runway model's look can be very unique and interesting. Whereas a print model must be very photogenic.

Runway modeling is done in various locations. Some department stores will do their own runway shows in their store. There are various producers, of which I am one, who will produce fashion shows for a client. These are usually very high-end shows. These charity shows raise money for their cause. The shows are luncheon or dinner shows set in large ballrooms. Example: City of Hope, AIDS Foundation, High Schools, etc.

Runway Shows are done across the United States for Fashion Week. These shows are also done in Paris, Milan, London and Japan, to name a few. Many runway models will travel to all of the Fashion Weeks to do the shows. Travel is part of a top model's life.

Requirements to be a Runway Model

A runway model must be tall; 5'9" – 5'11" is the normal range for height.
- Thin in stature
- Size 2-4
- Measurements to fit a size 2-4
- Have a good runway walk
- Attractive look
- Projection of attitude

Runway Training

It is imperative that a model knows how to walk and do the various turns on the runway and at the bottom of the runway. They also need to know how to remove jackets and gloves, and how to carry purses.

To do this, they need training from someone who is an expert coach. I have trained many models in person and online. I am known in Los Angeles, California, as a Runway Coach. Many of the agencies have hired me to train their models. I have also discovered, trained and placed models with agencies in Los Angeles.

STAGE AND RUNWAY VARIATIONS

There are numerous routines and ramps, each a bit different from the other. A good model is noted for her ability to feel at ease in any situation and this comes only with constant practice.

STAGE IDENTIFICATION

Upper Stage Right	Upper Stage Center	Upper Stage Left
WINGS Right Stage	Center Stage	Left Stage **WINGS**
Down Stage Right	Down Stage Center	Down Stage Left

RUNWAY IDENTIFICATION AND BASIC ROUTINES

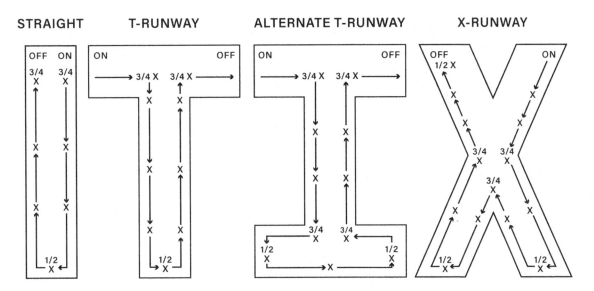

STRAIGHT   T-RUNWAY   ALTERNATE T-RUNWAY   X-RUNWAY

Key: 1/2x = half pivot   x = whole pivot   3/4 = three quarter pivot

Note: the length of the runway (and the commentary) will determine the number of pivots to execute. The number of pivots will always vary.

INFORMAL MODELING

There is a lot of this type of modeling that is executed in department stores across the US. A model will be hired to work in a specific part of the store to wear the clothing in that department to promote the sales. There is a platform at the front of the department that the model stands on, poses and attracts attention to that area as shoppers pass. The model may be asked to walk around the store holding a sign which has the designer's name printed on it. If customers ask questions such as price, the model interacts with them and provides information.

TEA ROOM MODELING

Some department stores have tea rooms or lunchrooms that they hire models to walk through to show customers what they are wearing. It is up to you, as the model, to know the price of the garment you are wearing and the fabrication, in case a customer asks. Never do you impose on their lunch unless they engage with you first.

FASHION WEEK

Fashion Week is usually twice a year. Many designers show their newest and latest collection at fashion week. All runway models want to work fashion week for the exposure and networking that it affords. Fashion week takes place across the United States and Europe. In Europe they call them couture collections and ready-to-wear collections.

CHARITY FASHION SHOWS

Charity Fashion Shows are usually executed in the ballroom of a hotel with a long runway and a stage.

Example: Vistas for Children does an annual show that I produce. I use a well-known couture designer and professional models. I also produce shows for various high school fundraisers.

PRIVATE SHOWS FOR DESIGNERS' CLIENTS —

Some designers will create private showings for their special clients. These are usually small intimate settings, so the clients can special order the clothing. The designer may also hold special appearances in department stores that carry their clothing line. Models are always hired for these events.

Suzanne Speaks

When I lived in NYC, my expertise was runway work. I would travel to Paris to do my fittings, then travel to Milan, Italy, for the collections there. Then, return to Paris to do the shows. After Paris, I would return to NYC to do the runway shows for Fashion Week. Many models go to Miami for the Swim Fashion Week shows as well. To be a top model, travel is part of your life.

TIPS

When you are young and living at home with your parents, you should be training as much as you can. If your parents are supportive, take as many classes as you can. Singing, dancing, acting and modeling. Even if you don't plan to be a singer, it is good to learn in case an acting roll presents itself and you are required to sing and carry a tune.

Try to go to events that happen to be in your area to see a fashion show. You can learn a lot by sitting in the audience.

Work on your own personal style to be unique.

Watch the shows from Paris, NYC and LA online to stay current with fashion and watch how the models perform.

Be sure to know of the designers who are in your area. Also, try to have your agent send you to meet with the people who book the shows for the department stores. They are in the Special Events department of the store.

Q & A

What do brands and designers look for when they are casting?

Designers, coordinators and producers are looking for models that align with the brand. Some designers may want models that are edgy and have tattoos. Designers that create couture evening dresses may want a model with a small bustline, no tattoos, and a sense of elegance. If they are casting for a Runway Show, the model has to have a good walk. When casting for print, they are looking for a model who has the "look" for their collection. The models must photograph well and move well in front of the camera, and at the same time exude facial expressions with attitude that aligns with the clothing brand. For example, the brand may be Athletic Wear. In this case, casting people are looking for athletic body types who are a bit more curvy and fit.

It is up to the model to produce a zed card that shows the model's attributes, so that when the agent submits them for the job, the client can look at the photos and say, "This model has the look I want for my collection. I want to see them in person."

I'm 12 years old and I want to be a model. Do I need to be a certain height?

No, at 12 years old you do not need to be a certain height. Height pertains much more to the model who is 16 and up. What you do need to be is a certain size. When the breakdown comes out for a model in your age range, it will say what size model they are looking for. As long as you fit that description, then your agent will submit you for the job.

When I was 12 years old, I was very tall for my age. I had not discovered modeling yet at 12, but my height proved to be an asset to me when I got older and had an interest in modeling. I am 5'11" and I worked in New York City, Europe and California for a span of 40 years as a model.

My daughter is 11 years old and is competing in modeling at a convention. Should she be walking in high heels for the audition at the modeling convention?

The answer to this question is no. Eleven-year-olds are booked as kids. And kids should audition like kids. By the time she is 13, she should begin to learn how to walk in heels.

CHAPTER 2

PRINT MODELING

What types of print modeling are available to a model?

There are many different types of print work for a model. In this chapter, I explain the various types of print jobs available to a model.

REQUIREMENTS FOR A PRINT MODEL ———

A print model does not have to be as tall as a runway model. A print model can be 5'8". This is the perfect size for a model to do ready-to-wear print.

The definition of ready-to-wear is: clothing that hangs in department stores and is made to fit the general public. That is why a print model can be shorter than a runway model, because the sizes are skewed to fit the overall public right off the hanger.

The print model needs to be photogenic, which means that the camera loves their face. The look of the print model is more welcoming. They have a friendly feel about them. Afterall, when you see clothing on a print model in a magazine, the look of the model helps to sell the garment that she is wearing.

COMMERCIAL PRINT ———

Commercial Print is when you are the model being used as a "prop" so to speak, to advertise or promote a product or location.

Example: If you are booked to wear a bathing suit and to be photographed with a few other models in an above ground swimming pool, this would be labeled commercial print. Why? Because you are used as a "prop" to what they are selling, which is the pool.

Another example: Let's say that AT&T booked you to be photographed holding a smartphone as if you are talking on it. This print advertisement is to sell the phone, and you as the model are secondary, used as a "prop" to the phone.

EDITORIAL PRINT ———

Editorial Print is found toward the back of a fashion magazine such as Vogue, Bazaar or Seventeen. The magazine features a photographer for that issue of the magazine. The editor and stylist who work for the magazine create a fashion story of various fashion statements and looks to be photographed for that issue of the magazine. The style of these photos is usually very creative and highly stylized, showing the new looks for the season, be it fall, winter, spring or summer.

It is a really big deal for a model to be featured in the editorial portion of a magazine. Usually, this kind of print work does not pay a very high rate. But the exposure is priceless. The model benefits by working with one of the top photographers in the business, and she gets tear sheets from a prestigious magazine.

In most cases, a prestigious magazine does not pay the model or the celebrity to be on the cover of the magazine. This is because it is so prestigious, and the exposure is such a great reward to either a model or celebrity.

CATALOGUE PRINT

This is easily definable. There are companies who sell their clothing by hiring models to be photographed in the clothing they manufacture, and then publish a catalogue that is distributed to a wide span of people across the country. This type of print modeling is very steady work for a model. In NYC there are companies that are called catalogue houses. The catalogue houses are hired to photograph and package catalogues for many different companies.

Here is an example: Lane Bryant has brick and mortar stores, and they also publish a catalogue. This company, Lane Bryant, hires a catalogue house that has a photographer, stylist and casting director who does the work for them. After the photos are finished, they send the photo and layout to the printing company who does the final production of the catalogue.

Many times, the catalogue house will track the number of sales of each garment sold that a model is wearing in their catalogue. If her percentage of sales are high, then they will hire her over and over. This is particularly true in Germany. They will pay the model who has high sales percentages large sums of money just to be sure they can secure her to work for them.

PRINT ADVERTISING CAMPAIGNS

These photos are throughout magazines and are considered print campaigns. The company promoting their product purchases advertising space in the magazines.

To be the Revlon Girl or the model who does Cover Girl, you would be contracted for a period of one to five years. For that duration of time when a model is signed to an exclusive contract, she is not allowed to work for any other client or competitor. Also, when a model is connected to the same product for several years as the "face" of that product line, the model becomes overexposed and traditionally other companies do not want to hire this model as she is thought of as the "Revlon Girl" or "Cover Girl." With this knowledge, the agent would negotiate a very hefty contract on behalf of the model. This model's career may be over after her contract expires, having been the face of such a campaign, with extreme exposure. No worries here, as landing such a lucrative campaign this model will be set for life. The model can transition her career into acting or hosting.

WEBSITE PRINT

Most clothing manufacturers and showrooms need to have photos taken of their current collection for the season. Spring, summer, fall, winter and transition. These photos are posted on the showrooms' websites so that the buyers can have an overall preview of the clothing line. The manufacturers of the clothing line may sell from their website as well.

PROMOTIONAL MODELING

For this type of modeling, there is no height requirement. Having a good look and friendly personality are the two requirements that are needed. This type of modeling is done at trade shows, car dealerships, malls and cosmetic departments. The job of the model is to hand out flyers or to welcome people to the trade show booth or car dealership. This type of modeling does not pay as much as print or runway.

SHOWROOM MODELING

In the national and regional fashion markets, there are showrooms that represent several designers' clothing. During markets which are usually five times a year for three to four days, the showroom will hire models to try on clothing for the buyers who come to their showroom, so that the buyer can see the fit of the clothing.

I have always liked doing showroom modeling and have done it throughout my career. Some models do not like doing it because the day rate is much lower than print. However, by doing showroom work, I met many designers, and in the end, they hired me to be photographed in their clothing.

I still today work in a showroom during markets and wear the clothing but transitioned into selling the product as well. For more than a decade, I worked for a clothing line as the "face" of their company and traveled to all of the markets in the US to wear and sell their collection. These markets are Chicago, Dallas, Atlanta, New York, Los Angeles, Minneapolis and Las Vegas.

FASHION PRINT

Fashion print is anything that has to do with fashion. This means clothing, jewelry, hats, gloves, outerwear, ski clothing, sunglasses, athletic wear, swimwear, purses, shoes and all fashion accessories.

LIFESTYLE MODELING

Lifestyle modeling is when people are photographed doing something that relates to life. The models are usually wearing clothing that one would wear in that particular lifestyle setting.

Example: Boating or walking on the beach. If someone is booking a lifestyle shoot for sailing, they may be selling a certain brand of clothing that people wear when they go sailing. They will photograph people on a boat wearing that clothing, and it will become an advertisement in a published magazine.

Lifestyle photos are usually photographed with the models being camera unaware. This means that the models never look at the camera while the photographer is taking the pictures. The models are relating to each other. For instance, they may be walking on the beach hand in hand while the photographer captures candid shots. Ralph Lauren was the designer who first started lifestyle advertising for his collection.

FIT MODELING

A fit model is a model who has the perfect measurements for a designer to fit their designs. This model is very important to a designer. Their measurements have to be exact for their sample sizes.

Example: From the bone at the back of your neck to the waist, the measurement must be specific to their design. The bust/waist/hip measurements are important as well as the length of the arms.

A fit model is usually about 5'8" to 5'9". A fit model can work every day with more than one designer and can make a very good living without ever putting her makeup on. It's all about the model's body. I have a friend who is a fit model for a junior brand and a missy clothing brand. She has been doing it for a long time. She is in her 50s now. As long as she stays fit and keeps her measurements perfect, she can work forever. There are a few agencies in Los Angeles that specialize in fit modeling.

HAND MODELING

Hand modeling can be very lucrative if you have the right size hand, and your hands have no marks, dark spots or scars. It is also a plus if your veins do not show too much on the back of your hand.

With so much technology trending today, hand modeling has become big business for some models. For example, when a company is advertising a smartphone, they need a model to hold it as if they are talking on the phone. The smartphone is the focus, but the hand must be attractive to the eye and the right size to hold the product.

TRAINING FOR COMMERCIALS, ACTING (TV & FILM), HOSTING

As a model it is important that you take a commercial class so that you can learn how to handle copy. Many times, when a company is doing an advertising campaign, they want the model to do both the print and the commercial which relates to the product that is being advertised. You must know how to do both - move in front of the camera for the print portion of the campaign, and also know how to deliver a commercial for the on-air advertising part of the campaign.

Models should not limit themselves to just runway and print modeling. It is important to be well-rounded and learn to act in commercials, take acting classes and hosting workshops.

Suzanne Speaks

MORE THAN MODELING

I personally have reinvented myself many times over. I started as a model and traveled the world, transitioned into acting (movies and commercials), and later became a producer. I'm so passionate about modeling, which led me to produce fashion shows and mentor upcoming models, to ensure that they have the tools they need for long-lasting careers.

TIPS

L Having music to put you in the mood for taking photos in the studio is a great help.

L Remember that modeling is a short-lived career, so always be preparing and studying for your next step.

L Find a catalogue with photos of models and copy the poses. Be aware of where their hands are placed in the photo. Study the expressions on their faces.

L Contact me for modeling classes (info in About the Author). I do a six-week online class for runway and print.

Q & A

What types of modeling should a beginner do? Commercial Print or Runway?

Any type of modeling is good for someone who is new to the business. Once you are signed with an agent, they will guide you and get you out on auditions. The idea is to make money. It really doesn't matter if it is a runway job or a print job. If you do not book jobs, then no one makes any money. This is a business. Many times, models forget this. Models must be realistic and know that the agent is happiest when their models are working. He has bills to pay, as do you. The modeling business isn't about having a fun hobby. It is work and it is a business.

Can being a model get you into other avenues of the entertainment business such as acting or commercials? Is it good to start with just modeling?

If you were to Google the top 20 models in the world, you would find that at least half of them have gone on to do commercials as well as become actors. Modeling does not have a long lifespan in the national markets. By the time you are in your early 30s, work begins to decline in the national markets. However, you can still work in the regional markets. NYC is a national market. Los Angeles and Chicago are examples of regional markets. It is impossible to make a living in LA just working as a model. You have to do it all to make a living at it. So, it is imperative that you are studying acting for commercials, TV and film. Some top models, such as Heidi Klum, parlayed their careers into hosting reality shows that are based on the modeling business. There are classes to take to learn hosting as well.

How do you get training or take classes to help you improve and get noticed in the industry?

If you need more runway training or print training to work in front of the camera, the agents will suggest a coach. I work with most of the agencies in LA. When they have girls that need training for runway, they call me. In fact, I have placed many models with agencies. I have trained them to walk and produced their zed cards. Then I walked them into agencies to be seen for representation. I pretty much package the model. Agents in LA know this about me and always welcome a call from me if I have a new model that I have trained. It saves the agent a lot of time as the model is ready to audition and work.

What does it mean when someone tells me that my son or daughter should be doing print work?

Usually this means that your son or daughter is very good looking and very photogenic. Also, your son or daughter is most likely very expressive and animated.

What does it mean to be photogenic?

When a photo is taken of a person, the light hits the face in certain ways. If you have high cheekbones, it is a plus. The light of the camera likes that shape. Light bounces off the shape of the face which reflects in the photograph. So, when someone says that you are very photogenic, it usually means that the camera loves the angles of your face and you take very good pictures. This is why high cheekbones on a model are very advantageous. People would tell me often that I am very photogenic. I have very high cheekbones and an angular face. It took me awhile to realize that people thought that I looked better in a photo than I did in person. This happens to be true when people tell you that you are very photogenic.

How does a model learn to work in front of a camera?

The best way to learn to work in front of the camera is to work with a trained coach or photographer. I teach this in the model classes, both online and in-person.

Can I still do print jobs if I have braces?

Yes, you can, no worries here. If the client is looking for someone age specific for their print campaign, then braces may be required for their shoot and it's a plus. I have used many young kids who have braces in my fashion shows. Please do not try to hide the fact that you have braces by not smiling. Braces are a part of almost every teen's life. It is worth the effort when they are off.

Does a model get to keep the clothing after a photo shoot?

If you are booked for a photo shoot and the client is paying you your hourly rate for the shoot, you will not be given any clothing after the shoot. However, if a designer contacts you or your agent and is looking to do a barter or trade, then you will get clothing in exchange for doing the photo shoot. This type of arrangement can be very lucrative to the model. You get paid in clothing and the designer will usually let you have access to the photos after the shoot, so that you can use them on your zed card or in your portfolio.

CHAPTER 3

OVERSEAS MODELING

Why travel to Europe to work as a model?

Some of the most talented designers and photographers are in Europe. There are also more fashion magazines in each country in Europe versus the US. Therefore, there is more opportunity for a model to work and get tear sheets for their portfolios, which gives a model more credibility.

SUZANNE'S EUROPE STORY ————————

I was represented by Wilhelmina Agency in New York City. Willy, as we called her, kept pushing for me to go to Europe. She told me that it would be good for me to go to Europe to get my book together, so that when I came back to NYC she could promote me better. The experience and tear sheets would give a boost to my career.

I had every excuse in the world not to do this. I didn't speak the language and I had a life in NYC. Basically, I was afraid. I didn't arrive in NY until I was 22 years old. I went for a modeling convention called Model Association of America (MAA). It was held at the Waldorf Astoria Hotel. After that convention, I stayed in NYC and began my modeling career. It wasn't easy in the beginning, and I split my time between trying to be a model and also working part-time jobs to pay bills.

When I was 25 years old, I married a well-known Art Director for Revlon in NYC. The marriage did not last but a year. After the divorce things seemed to change for me. I developed a much tougher skin and even though I was a working model in NYC, I was determined to put my personal life aside and focus on my career. My mindset had changed, and I decided that I wanted to be a well-known top model in NYC. I was 26 years old. I knew that I had to focus because the modeling business is only kind to the young, and I was already behind the ticking clock.

I talked to my agent Willy about going to Paris to work, and she said that she could set things up for me. She would be my Mother Agent and make the introductions. While she was in the process of doing this, Monsieur Givenchy came to NY to look for American models to be in his show for the Couture Collections in Paris. I really prepared for this audition. I truly looked like I had just stepped out of a magazine when I walked into the audition. The Parisian designers hold their auditions in a very different way than we do in the States. He had all the models show up at the same time. He was a very tall man, so he looked over the sea of models in the room and began pointing at the models that he said he wanted to stay. There were what seemed to be over 100 or so models in that room. He pointed to me. And to be sure that he meant me, I pointed back to myself and said, "Do you mean me?" In his French accent he said, "Oui, oui," which means "yes, yes" in English. These were the first French words I learned. He then asked all of the other models to leave. There were about six of us left after all of the rest had cleared the room. We were the chosen few.

He began to take measurements and had his assistant jot them down. He didn't even have us walk for him. Somehow, he just knew who he wanted and which models inspired him by their "look." To have been handpicked and working with the master himself, Givenchy, was a very big deal. I really didn't realize how big a deal it was until after I arrived in Paris and was a model in his show.

When I arrived in Paris, I met with the agent that Willy had arranged for me to meet. They signed me. Most of my time was spent in fittings with Monsieur. He would begin with bolts of fabric and drape the fabric on me. Eventually, he made patterns out of muslin. I would stand for hours as he draped and pinned. He also asked me my opinion about the garment he was making. I loved to engage with him on this. Soon it was showtime. Each model wore two garments in the show. He chose me to be the first model to walk in the show and I was the last model to close the show. Opening and closing the show was a feather in my cap. I walked down the runway in a beautiful evening gown with a big Standard Poodle. That was all it took. After that show every designer in Paris wanted to book me for their shows the next season. Also, the photographers were calling the agency in Paris to book me for the editorial print in the magazines. The rest is history.

I went back and forth between Paris and NY every six weeks. The only thing I focused on was my career. I accomplished what I set out to do. When you begin hearing that casting is putting out a breakdown saying that they are looking for models who are the same type as Suzanne Von Schaack, you know that you have arrived. On one of my trips back to New York in my downtime between seasons, I discovered acting. I decided that I wanted to stay in NYC and take classes at the William Esper Studio, studying the Meisner Method. This was another stroke of luck for me, as Mr. Esper used myself and another actor as an experiment to train in private sessions with a teacher he had trained. Her name is Joanne Baron. I was her first student. Joanne has become a renowned acting coach in Los Angeles at the Baron Brown Studio. All of my agents and the designers in Paris and Milan were furious with me. They couldn't believe that I would not come back for the collections that season.

I had been back and forth between Europe and traveled to Hong Kong for several years. For me it was time to try to conquer something else and acting was "IT" for me. After studying acting in NYC for a couple years, I began to work as an actress. My first movie was *Tootsie*. Later, I worked in Woody Allen's film *Zelig* and in Fred Williamson's film *The Last Flight*. Then I was off to Los Angeles for pilot season. I returned from that trip to NYC, sold everything in my apartment, and moved to Los Angeles to work as a model and try my hand at an acting career.

Suzanne Speaks

My modeling career really took off after I went to Europe to work with Givenchy. It is easier to get published work in Europe that provides you tear sheets to build your portfolio, because there are so many publications.

TIPS

- Each country, France, Italy, London, Germany all have their own fashion magazines and there are many, many publications.

- Fashion trends originate in Europe first. The designers in the US follow the European trends for fashion.

- In the US we have only a handful of fashion magazines, making it harder to get tear sheets.

Q & A

What Makes a Super Model?

There are a number of things that contribute to making a Super Model "Super." It is usually a combination of their walk, their eyes, hair, body shape, personality, confidence, the way they photograph, how they speak and their personal style.

It is Important to Take Good Care of Yourself.

Take care of your body, spirit and mind. Have a plan and a purpose for each day. Through self-care, the light that shines within you can be seen brightly by others. If you are run down and tired, it will show. The world is full of people, if you want to stand out and be exceptional, then you have to take care of "you." Eat right, get proper rest, be a ray of sunshine wherever you go, and feed your mind with beautiful and powerful thoughts.

Be Who You Are.

We are all different and diverse in ethnicity and nationality. It is important that as human beings that we all get along and have respect for one another. There are leaders and there are followers. Always strive to be a leader! Allow your personality, kindness and understanding to be shown to others. Create your own style in the way you dress. Brush up on your communication skills. Lend a helping hand when you can. Know who you are and what your values are, and people will notice.

Talent.

Expand. Take a lot of classes for your own personal development. Don't stop at being a model. Be a singer, dancer, actor, musician, athlete and artist. Do it all. A well-rounded person is a happy person.

Get Involved.

Try out for a play. Offer to work backstage. Participate in group activities. Be sure that you are the first to introduce yourself to new people that you meet so that you are remembered.

Practice Makes Perfect.

Create your own Fashion Show to entertain your family and friends. Sing to everyone or showcase somewhere. Perform in dance recitals. Ask a friend to take photos of you in a park or find a photographer that will do test shots with you for practice. Find a good commercial class. Try different ways of doing your makeup and hair each day.

What's New and Current.

Be sure to keep up with the new trends in fashion. Be a trendsetter and create your own look and style. Read the fashion magazines. Research "who are the top 10 models in the world." Go online and watch the Designer Fashion Shows so you know what a Super Model looks like.

CHAPTER 4

FINDING AN AGENT

How does a model find an agent to represent them?

This question is one I get asked over and over. There are many different avenues to follow to make this happen. But it isn't that easy to get an agent.

REFERRAL

Being referred by a friend, photographer, stylist or producer is usually the best way to meet an agent. Relationships in this industry are supreme. If someone who personally knows a good agent is willing to recommend you to them, you have just been blessed.

OPEN CALLS

Some agencies have open calls once a month to find new talent. As a model, it's up to you to do the research and find out which agencies in your city represent models. There are a lot of agencies in LA, Chicago, NY, Miami, Dallas, etc. But it is up to the model to research online and find out which ones represent models for print and runway. Once you have done that, you can make a plan of action. Find out when they hold their open calls and then go.

SUBMISSIONS

You can submit online to an agent. This is kind of a shot in the dark. Agents get hundreds of submissions daily.

MODELING CONVENTION

There are several conventions such as IPOP, IMTA, MAAI and others who scout for new talent. If they feel that you have the "It Factor," for a fee they will offer you the opportunity to go to their convention. At the convention, you work with many professionals in the modeling, acting, singing and dance world. You have the opportunity to perform in front of about 100 plus agents and managers who are looking for new talent to sign with their agency. For those who do not live in LA, NYC or a major city, this is a great way to put yourself in front of agents and people who can help you.

ON THE JOB

When you meet people along your way, at trainings or doing a job, be sure to ask those you meet, even another model, if they might introduce you to an agent they might know.

WHERE TO LIVE AND WHERE TO HAVE AN AGENT

Next Steps – Contracts

As a model you will want to position yourself to live in a city where there is a lot of opportunity to work as a model. If you are young and not of majority age, you may not want to move to LA or NY until you are 18 years old. At that time, you can think about college and perhaps position yourself to go to school in a city where you can also model. It is difficult to get an agent in NY or LA if you do not live there.

The other option is to test the waters and go to NYC during fashion week for the shows. You can rent an Airbnb for a few weeks. Go to the auditions for the shows and go to open calls to meet agents while you are there. If you like NYC, then you can make more solid plans to move if you like.

What does an agent do for me when I join them?

The job of an agent is to submit you for modeling opportunities in which you fit the criteria. This is how it works. Once you are represented by an agent, you are allowed to be on LA Casting. This is a site that is on the internet that all agents and casting are connected to. Your agent will ask you to provide them with two photos of yourself. With LA Casting, you are allowed to upload two pictures for free once you are represented by a legitimate agent. All legitimate agents are required to hold a license with the state that they do business. If you want to put more pictures on LA Casting than the two that are free you can, but you are charged $10.00 for each additional photo.

Your agent pays for breakdowns to be sent to them on a daily basis each month. Breakdowns are only issued to agents. Your agent may have other relationships with clients that specifically book their models through their agency. When the agent sees a job in the breakdowns that are specific to your age, ethnicity and size, they will send one of your pictures that are on LA Casting to the casting director. Keep in mind that there are over 400 agents and managers in LA that are submitting their talent for the same job opportunity. All of these submissions are looked at by the client or casting director.

Your photo is usually about the size of a thumbnail print seen on the client's computer screen with all of the other models that were submitted. The casting director clicks on the photos that she likes, which is then sent to each respective agent to have that model come to the audition where they are seen in person.

The competition is really fierce. Usually, each agent submits at least 3-5 talent to each casting. Do the math. If there are 400 agents submitting 5 models from each agency for this casting, then the casting director is receiving 2,000 model submissions. Out of these, the casting director may choose anywhere from 30 to 50 models that they will see for the job. In some cases, like a runway show, they may need 20 plus models. But for a print job they may only need to book one female and one male model.

CHILDREN'S AGENCIES IN LOS ANGELES, CALIFORNIA

1. Abrams Artist Agency
2. CESD Talent Agency
3. Mavrick Artist Agency
4. Coast to Coast Talent Group
5. LA Models LA Talent
6. Paloma Model & Talent
7. Zuri Model & Talent
8. Brand Model & Talent
9. Daniel Hoff Agency
10. Clear Talent

FIT AGENCIES IN LOS ANGELES, CALIFORNIA

1. Rage Models
2. MPM Models and Talent Inc. (Full Service Agency including fit models and plus models)

TOP AGENTS IN LOS ANGELES, CALIFORNIA ——————————

1. LA Models
2. Q Model Management
3. Bella Agency
4. CESD
5. Wilhelmina Models
6. Aston Models & Talent
7. Elite Model Management
8. IMG Models
9. Ford Models
10. Next Models
11. Luft Agency (formerly Wunder Models)

Note: Rates in Los Angeles vary from $100/hour to $200/hour
Or day rates $1,500 - $3,000 per day

TOP AGENTS IN NEW YORK CITY ——————————

1. New York Model Management
2. Wilhelmina Models
3. IMG Models
4. Q Model Management
5. Elite Model Management
6. Ford Models
7. Next Management
8. VNY Models
9. Red Models
10. Ohlsson Model & Talent (represents children to work in Chicago, Austin/Dallas and NYC)

Note: Rates in NYC are $350/hour to $400/hour

Suzanne Speaks

If you sign with an agent but you are not going out for auditions, you may need different photos. If you do new photos and you are still not getting auditions, then you have the right under the terms of the contract after a 90-day period of no auditions or work, to terminate the contract and move on. I would not terminate the contract until you have secured another agent.

I live in LA and I have trained many young girls who want to be models. I have taught them to walk for runway and how to move in front of the camera. I have also set up their photo shoots with the right photographer and helped them produce their zed cards. Then I have found them agents. There aren't a lot of people like me around, but if you find a mentor who can help you, go for it.

TIPS

- Do not leave an existing agent or manager without having another one already lined up.

- Talk to your agent regarding your career before you just opt to leave. You may not be getting out because your photos are not working.

- It is best to try to do everything you can to make things work before you change agents or managers; it is not good for your reputation to hop from one agency to another on a regular basis.

- Your pictures are your best tool. Keep them current and representative of you and how you look. If you cut your hair, you will need to do new photos.

- If you are asked to audition in person, be sure that you have prepared and show up to your audition looking like a bright shiny penny. No excuses.

- Your skin, nails, hair and clothing must all be in tip top shape.

- If you choose to wear a color, be sure that it enhances your skin tone. Some colors do not look good on some people.

- This is your chance to meet a new client not only for this opportunity, but also for work in the future. So, bring on your best attitude!

- Be sure you have your zed card! You must have a zed card to leave with the client so that they can remember you and also have your stats.

Q & A

When you're interviewing for an agency, how do you determine which one is the best to go with?

When you are shopping for an agent, you pretty much have to go with your gut feeling and rely on the research that you have done pertaining to them. The relationship between an agent and a model should be a good partnership. It has to be a good fit and equally balanced. Both of you should show excitement to be joining together for the common goal of making money. If a very large well-known agency wants to sign you and you are very new, it might not be a good fit, as you may get lost in the shuffle. The girls that have been around awhile and have experience are usually the priority over someone new. Models that are seasoned are easier to sell to the client. You'll want to do your homework. If your focus is runway modeling, then you need to know which agencies book the bulk of the runway shows in the city where you have your agent. Some agencies are not strong in the runway department.

Should I sign an exclusive or non-exclusive contract?

Some agencies sign you across the board. Or you can choose to tell the agent that you only want to be represented for modeling. It is my opinion that it is best to diversify and have another agent for commercials and yet another agent for theatrical (TV and movies). However, if you are just starting out and you do not have any training or experience doing commercials, TV and movies, you may wish to let your modeling agent submit you in these fields, while you are studying these crafts. In LA there is a lot of non-union commercial work which helps the newer commercial actor to gain experience. The bigger commercials, TV and movies are usually union jobs, but if you are not a member of SAG/AFTRA, then you cannot do those jobs. Having said that, there are many non-union jobs for TV/Film and commercials that are available. If you are signed with an agency in LA, you can also have an agent in NY or other cities. This means that you are exclusive in LA, but free to have other agents in other cities.

How does your agency determine what you're submitted for, and if your size, measurements and height are right for the job? Being athletic can show you weigh more due to muscle mass.

Your agent has several of your photos uploaded on their site for submission. If you have a good bathing suit body, your agent will ask you for those types of photos so that you can be submitted for that type of work. I personally was not a bathing suit model. At 5'11" my proportions were not right. I was very long waisted. Usually, the models who are 5'8" or tops 5'9" are best for swim. Also, I had very light skin and not much of a bust. Clients prefer models who have olive or darker skin tone for swim.

The size that is required to work for couture designers is size 2-4. That is the size of the designer's samples. Some showrooms will have samples in a size 6 or 8. But most use a size 4 as their gauge.

If you have a very athletic body, you can still work doing activewear, swim, ready-to-wear and couture, as long as you fit the clothing. If you do not fit the clothing and you are too muscular, then something will have to give. If modeling is what you want to do, then you may have to lean out if you are too muscular. Your agent will receive feedback from the clients and talk to you regarding future castings.

How do you know when to switch agents or managers?

If you have been with an agent or a manager and you are not getting any auditions during the season when it is most busy, then it is time to find a new one. If you have signed a contract, and the contract is not up yet, there are no worries. There is usually an out clause in the contract that states that if you have not booked any work within a three-month period of time, then the contract is null and void. All you need to do is to send a certified letter to the agent or manager stating that you would like to terminate your contract and representation.

CHAPTER 5

PHOTOS, ZED CARD & PORTFOLIO

How important is it for a model to have current photos?

Photos are the most important tool that a model can have. Photos are sent electronically by your agent to casting. If your photos are not up to par, you will not get called in for the audition.

PHOTOS

Photos in your portfolio are important. When you go to a casting for a print job, the client will ask to see your portfolio. If you have tear sheets in your portfolio, it is a plus. Work begets work. Clients feel more comfortable when they see that other clients have invested their money in you by hiring you to do their advertising campaign. If you are just starting out and you do not yet have tear sheets in your portfolio, then ten great photos of you from various photo shoots will be a good start.

- It is very important that you have a zed card to leave with the client who is casting. If you do not have a zed card, then you will seem unprofessional.
- If you change your hair, you need new photos and a new zed card.
- Choose colors in clothing that enhance your eye color and the color of your skin tones. Not all colors look good on all people.
- Do not use clothing that have logos on them for your photo shoots. It is very distracting and takes away from you.
- It is best to use solid colors for your photo shoots. Clothing that is too busy looking will distract from you.

ZED CARD

The zed card for a model is equivalent to your business card. It is a selection of photos that are produced into a card that the model leaves with the client at an audition. This card has a headshot on the front and 4 photos on the back. When you put a zed card together, it is up to you as the model to decide how to market yourself. That will determine the type of photos and clothing you will choose to accent your strengths as a model.

- Do some photos smiling and some with no smile.
- If you do not have a body type for swim, do not do photos in a bathing suit for your card.
- Choose clothing that makes you stand out. The colors you choose to wear in your photos are very important. Not all colors are good on all skin tones.
- The eyes have it. It is imperative to wear a color that enhances your eyes and your skin tone so that your eyes pop in the photos.

Types of Photos that Should be used for a Zed Card

- You will need a headshot on the front of your card.
- You will need four photos on the back of your card.
- If you have a good swimsuit body then you should have a photo of yourself in a swimsuit.
- Have a casual shot of yourself in a jean outfit.
- Have a shot in something a bit dressy.
- Have a shot that shows you having fun. Riding a bicycle, dressed in cut-off jeans or skateboarding in a cute outfit.

PORTFOLIO

A portfolio is a book that is filled with acetate sheets for you to put photos and tear sheets to be displayed. When you go on auditions for print jobs, you take your portfolio with you so that you can let the client view your work. Your photos also allow the client to see how you photograph.

With the technology of today's world, many models will upload their photos on their iPad for clients to view instead of using a portfolio. It is less expensive to use an iPad, because you do not have to print the photos for your portfolio. However, there are mixed reviews about using an iPad versus a portfolio. It is best that once you are signed with an agent to check to see what your agent prefers. Every region and market will be different regarding this choice.

8x10 PHOTO

An 8x10 photo is a headshot of you with your resume attached to the back. Your 8x10 photo is usually used for acting. A zed card is used for modeling.

TEST SHOOTS WITH PHOTOGRAPHERS

Test shoots are usually done in a barter type situation. The photographer wants to experiment with lighting or a new lens and the model needs photos, so they collaborate together. When a model first starts in their early beginnings, they need photos in their portfolio for clients to view when they go on auditions. By doing test shoots you gain experience and photos for your portfolio.

SUZANNE VON SCHAACK

Height: 5'9.5" Bust: 34b Waist: 26 Hips: 36 Size: 4-6 Shoe: 9 Hair: blonde Eyes: green

Suzanne Speaks

Remember that when your agent is submitting you for a job, the photo that pops up on the casting director's screen is only thumbnail size, so it is important that the color of the shirt or top you are wearing makes your eyes pop in the photo. Also, the color you are wearing must compliment your skin tone.

To be a model you also have to know how to pose in front of a camera. There are many things to learn about working in a studio and posing. If you're just starting out, have a friend take photos of you. Another way to learn how to pose for photos is to hire a professional photographer to shoot your photos for your zed card. A good professional photographer will work with you to help with your posing, expressions and mood of the photo.

TIPS

Time is money. It is imperative for you to be able to move easily and in a fluid way to get the shot quickly.

Hands that are not in the right place or that are not elegant to the eye can ruin a photo.

Bad foot placement can also ruin a photo. However, feet can be cropped out. Hands cannot.

As you pose, be sure to stay on your mark so that you are always in focus.

Know the best angles for your face to be photographed.

Q & A

HOW TO FIND YOUR LOOK

What is your advice for finding brands that match with your "look?"

I would suggest that you brainstorm with your agent to try to identify clients that might be able to use your type with your "look" for either catalogue work or advertising campaigns. Agents have clients that they work with on a regular basis or seasonally. The agents know who these people are and have developed working relationships with them. Agents also have relationships with casting directors who are responsible for casting various types of jobs. This is why a model wants to be with an agency, because the agent receives the daily breakdowns for jobs and many times is on a first name basis with many clients.

Does print work pay more than Runway Shows?

Typically, the answer to this is yes. Each market has different pay scales. In NYC, which is a national market, many models are paid $300 – $400 per hour as a very handsome rate. In LA, the rate for print is $150 – $200 per hour. Unless it is a big campaign. Then, the model can be paid several thousand dollars.

CHAPTER 6

AUDITIONING "YOU HAD ME AT HELLO"

What is the most important thing you should do to prepare for a casting?

It's all in your attitude! Showing up to an audition like a shiny penny is the goal. This doesn't happen overnight. Exercise, diet, perfect skin, pretty hair and nails happen because you take care of yourself on a daily, weekly, monthly basis.

WHAT DO I TAKE WITH ME TO AN AUDITION?

- Zed Card
- Portfolio or iPad
  Note – many models upload their photos onto their iPad for the client to view
- Model Bag – small version with proper undergarments/shoes
- Yourself looking fabulous from head to toe

You must have a zed card or at the very least an 8x10 headshot with your stats and name on it. This includes your height, bust, waist, hip measurements, shoe size, as well as your name and contact number of your agent. The client is usually seeing many models and without a photo or zed card the client will have nothing to reference at the end of the casting. If you do not have a zed card or photo to leave with the client who is casting, you will not have a chance of being booked for the job.

HOW SHOULD A MODEL DRESS FOR AN AUDITION?

YOU want to stand out! It is my preference for models to dress in all black when they come to an audition. Wearing all black makes YOU, the model, stand out. The client can see the shape of the model's figure and easily discern if the model is the right size for the designer's clothing. I prefer that the model wear skinny black jeans and a form fitting black top. The top can have some style to it, but it must show the model's figure. You can also wear black shorts with a black top in the summer and early fall for auditions when it is hot. For a print audition, you should dress according to what you are auditioning for.

Example: If the audition is for activewear, you should come dressed that way. If it is for swimwear, have a bathing suit with you. If it's for evening wear, just wear all black. Always bring heels and a flat shoe in case they have you try on clothing.

AUObjectTIONING FOR A RUNWAY SHOW ————

Locations: The audition could be in various locations. Here are some of them.

Your Agency – The client may prefer to hold the audition at your agency. I usually prefer this for my auditions when I am producing a show. The area provided to walk at the agency may be in the hall area, a roof top or within the agency office. Sometimes a lot of space for you to walk is provided and sometimes it is limited, so be prepared to adjust.

A Hotel – The client may be from out of town and may hold the audition where they are staying.

Atelier or Studio – A designer will usually hold the audition at their studio.

Music – Many times, the client does not provide music for the audition. The best way to prepare for this scenario is to practice to a certain song at home. Then when you audition and there is no music, you remember the beat of the music you have practiced with and you will be just fine. Music usually helps a model to pace her walk. When there is none, the model can be thrown off and her walk can be dragged down.

AUDITIONING FOR A PRINT JOB ————

The print audition can be held in various places depending on the job. Advertising agencies are hired by various brands to spearhead their advertising and marketing campaigns. Many times, a print audition is held at the ad agency with the art director who is in charge of the campaign.

Example: Grey Advertising at this time represents:
Gillette, Pantene, Volvo, Discover, Proctor & Gamble (P&G)

Other locations for a print audition may be the following:
- Photographer's Studio
- Casting Office
- The client may come to your Agency to cast
- Merchandising Mart in your city
- Designer's Studio
- Clothing Manufacturer's Factory Location
- Showroom

THE CALLBACK

A callback is when you are called back to be seen again, so the client can make their final decision. The client may have seen, for example, 100 models for the job. Out of the 100, they will narrow it down to maybe 10. From the 10 that they see on the callback, the client will confirm the models' availability for the dates they are booking, and then make a final decision on who they choose to cast for the job.

"On Hold" or "On Avail"

Many times, a callback doesn't happen. Some clients run a casting and at the end of the casting they will put several models "on hold" or "on avail". This means that the model's agent will confirm the model's availability to do the job on the date or dates that the client has chosen. After the client has received confirmation of the models' availability, the client will book the models of their choosing and release the other models that they did not choose from the "on hold" or "on avail".

DIRECT BOOKING

A direct booking is when a client books you sight unseen.

Here is an example: Your agent may have submitted your photo to a client who is doing a shoot or a runway show. The client may have booked you in the past and does not see the need to have to see you again in person, so they just book you without an audition.

Another example: The client may be from NYC but is shooting in California because the weather is better in the winter months in California than in NY. The client may choose to book models who live in California instead of flying models from NY. This client may ask your agent to send him submissions and then direct book you sight unseen for the job. When they arrive in California from NY, the first time you see the client will be on the set. Many times, your agent will have video footage that he has shot of you and will send that to them as well.

When I am booking models for fashion shows, I remember models that I have booked in the past and I just automatically book them again and do not need them to come to a casting. However, if I haven't seen a model for about a year, I will request them to come to the casting because sometimes a model can gain weight, change hair, etc.

GENERAL RULES FOR A MODEL ON THE SET

1. Always be on time or a little bit early. If you are late to a shoot that involves another model and your lateness causes everything to run over time, then you will be docked some of your pay. Lateness is not a good thing!

2. Bring a book to read so that you can sit quietly until they are ready for you to go into hair and makeup.

3. If you need to use the bathroom, let someone know where you are going, so they can find you if you are needed right away.

4. Always be friendly and nice to everyone.

5. Be sure to bring your personal model bag with deodorant and all of the things that you might need for personal hygiene, as well as the proper undergarments.

6. When you are finished with your hair and makeup, be careful so that you do not touch your face or hair. Also, be mindful of both your hair and makeup when you get dressed, so you do not get makeup on the clothing or mess up your hair.

7. At the end of the photo shoot, be sure to have your voucher signed. A voucher book will be given to you by your agency. This will have your start time and end time on it along with the name of the client. The client must sign your voucher. This serves as your invoice for doing the job.

8. Be sure to thank everyone that you have met on the set before you leave. You can ask if anyone would like your zed card or your business card.

9. You could also ask them for their business card.

10. If you do get the photographer's business card, the client's card as well as the makeup & hair team, write them a thank you note when you get home. Staying connected and grateful to people that you have worked with is always a good thing to do.

Suzanne Speaks

I have worked on both sides of the fence, as a model and now as a client, producing and casting shows. I did very well as a model and made a nice living at it for years. I was very professional and dependable. Now working as a producer casting models for shows, if a model comes in with nothing to leave me such as a zed card or headshot, I do not book her. I see 50 plus models in one casting. Without a picture with proper stats, I just can't remember them. Also, a model that comes to a casting without the proper tools such as heels and a zed card signals a red flag to me – unprofessional! For a print audition you will need your zed card and portfolio. It is usually not necessary to bring your portfolio to a runway audition. At a runway audition you will need a zed card to leave with the client.

When I am casting for a runway show, I am not looking at the clothing you wear to the audition. I am looking at your shape to be sure that you will fit the designer's clothing. If I am not sure, I always have a tape measure with me to take your measurements.

TIPS

- Remember that the client will be dressing you in what the designer or manufacturer is selling. So, it is best to be dressed in a way that you are like a clean canvas. Wear all black to an audition.

- It is important for a model to be aware of who the top advertising agencies represent. By knowing what brands they represent, you will be aware of the possible modeling jobs for you as a model.

- Be sure that your hair, nails and skin are in perfect shape as well as your pedicure.

- For models 15 years old and up, you should wear basic makeup.

➤ For kids who are 4 years up to 12 years, no makeup.

➤ For 13 and 14-year-olds, a bit of blush and clear lip gloss is perfect.

➤ Young girls under 13 should not wear heels to an audition.

➤ Wear the exact same outfit to your callback as you did to your first casting.

➤ Wear your hair exactly the same to your callback as you did your first audition.

➤ For a runway audition you will need to have heels (13 and older). At the audition the client will have you walk. It is not necessary to bring your portfolio. Please bring your zed card.

➤ Many times, casting will not have music for the audition. My suggestion is to practice at home to a song that has a good beat. Put that song on a CD and play it in your car before you get to the audition. This way, if there is no music, at least you can recall the beat of familiar music when you walk for the client.

➤ The music I use to train models is "4 Minutes" by Madonna, it has a good beat.

➤ Models that audition for me that do not have at least an 8x10 headshot with their stats on it, do not have a chance of getting booked by me. I prefer that the model is professional enough that she or he has a zed card to leave with me. If they do not have this, there is no way that I can possibly remember them.

➤ There is no excuse for a model to show up for a casting looking like a wreck. If I'm going to pay the model $200 per hour, I expect that they come looking like they have prepared for the audition.

Example: If you went to a store to buy a chair and it had scratches on it, would you pay full price for it? Of course, you wouldn't. Models must remember that he/she is the product that they are selling to the client who is hiring. If you do not look like you are perfect from head to toe, and you are not professional with a zed card and great walk, then casting may feel that you are not worth paying $200 per hour. Come prepared and well trained! Professionalism is key to winning the job.

 Do not wear plaid, bold prints or shirts with logos to an audition.

There is a very good product that you can use to bump up your tan. Sublime Bronze: Self-tanning towelettes by L'Oreal. I buy mine in medium color. They do a great job and your sunless tan looks natural. Use this if you are auditioning for swimwear or need to bump up your skin tone for spring clothing.

Q & A

What do I look for in a model when I am casting for a Fashion Show that I am producing?

As a producer, when I am auditioning a model there are basic things that I look for and they are the following:

1. Does the model look well put together? The model's hair, nails and skin must be in perfect shape.

2. Does the model have a good walk? Does the model know how to pose and then turn at the bottom of the runway in the right way?

3. Does the model come prepared wearing high heels? Is the model the right size for the designer's clothing? Is the model representative of the designer's brand?

4. Is the model professional and have a printed zed card?

5. Does the model have energy when they walk, or is the model's walk flat? By energy, I mean an attitude as well as some hip movement.

6. When I cast a fashion show, I am always looking to cast a variety of ethnicities and nationalities.

How did you deal with rejection and the mentally draining parts of modeling?

In the beginning of my modeling career in NYC, I had a lot of rejection. I had test shots in my portfolio and I was told that my arms were too long. What I eventually did to get it all together, was go to Europe and work there as a model and do what the other models did that had established themselves. They went to Europe and came back with a portfolio full of tear sheets from prestigious magazines, having worked with famous photographers and stylists.

When I returned to NY from Europe, I not only had a lot of experience and more confidence, but I was able to compete with more established models and my portfolio had tear sheets. Rejection is a part of the modeling and acting business. Every day you are looking for the next booking. A working model is a happy model. I developed this attitude toward things. I would go on the audition or casting and if I heard nothing, I just let it go. I would say to myself, "That was just not my job." I never took it personally. You can't really because there are so many variables to why the client chooses someone other than you. I just kept moving forward and eventually it would be me winning the job. And that happened more often than not. I knew that I was not a person who could punch a clock day after day. So, the rejection was easier to face than caving in and becoming a worker bee. I stuck with it and found my way working in various markets and made a very nice living as a model and traveled the world.

What is the most taxing part of modeling that a newcomer should expect to face?

There are two taxing parts of the modeling business. One is that there is a lot of waiting around between auditions. When it is the season for working, the auditions can be hard to keep up with. Then there is the downtime where you just sit and wait for the phone to ring. The second is being put on hold for a big job that you really want, and then receiving a call or email that you have been been released, which means that you did not get the job. Clients put models and actors on hold because they are not sure which model to go with. Many times, there are several people who have to agree on who gets the job.

Do most jobs pay for travel?

Yes! Most jobs will pay for your airfare. Some jobs will pay travel time or gas if you have to drive a great distance to get to the location of the job site. Your agent negotiates these details for you.

Is modeling seasonal?

Yes, it is seasonal in the US markets. It is very busy January through May. But, June, July and August are very slow months for modeling. It gets busy again in September through the beginning of December. During the summer months many models go to Japan, Spain, Miami, Paris or Milan to work.

SAFETY IN AUDITIONS

In terms of being the parent of an almost 18-year-old, what if there is a casting and my daughter has to go into a room with the casting person and I can't see what's going on?

Example: What if there's a guy in the room and they get inappropriate with her and I have no idea it's happening?

This question is something that every mother of a young girl or guy worry about. Even when your child goes off to college there are things and people to worry about. Usually, when your daughter/son goes on an audition, there will be other models going on the same audition so there is safety in numbers.

Most auditions are at casting centers. These are casting offices that rent out space to cast. Casting directors are hired by the client to hold the audition. These are very safe places. The business is very small, and everyone knows everyone that is "someone" in the business. People know that their reputation is important and are usually very ethical. This is why there are casting offices which the clients hire to run their auditions – for professionalism and safety.

My biggest worry in NYC was not who I was going to see for a job or meeting a photographer in their studio, but the stranger who got on the elevator with me. I always had my keys in between my fingers. I carried pepper spray in NYC, but never had to use it. At some point as a parent, you have to let your child become an adult and learn how to handle themselves and use good judgement. If anything should happen that seems inappropriate, your daughter/son should tell you as well as their agent. I never came across the "casting couch" thing in all of the cities and places that I traveled. I find that the girls that are on the periphery of the business may fall into that trap. They may not be represented by an agent and may answer modeling jobs online. But once you are represented by an agent, the castings that you are sent out on are real, and the client has to book a model to do the job and it is all "business."

I also took karate classes, both for exercise and to learn self defense. I always think that this is a good idea for any young woman. I loved my karate classes. Karate is very centering and I was in the best shape because of it. The added bonus was that I was not afraid because I knew that I could protect myself if I had to.

How does a parent properly protect their aspiring model from exploitation or potentially unhealthy comments / behaviors while not interfering with the casting, work, etc., the model is involved in?

As a parent who is managing their child who is under 18 years old, it is your duty to ask questions and be sure that your daughter/son is not being exploited and treated in a disrespectful way. Some casting people can be harsh. It is best to be represented by an agent that you can talk to regarding any issues. Once the model is 18, he or she must be strong enough to speak up for themselves if any monkey business is going on. When I was modeling, I had a couple situations that I had to deal with but nothing that I couldn't handle. Your Agent is your protector. They know the good people in the business and usually, they also know the ones to stay away from. So, follow their lead. But if anything goes down that isn't right or is questionable behavior, then report it to your agent. Know the guidelines of a booking before you take it. If you are to travel for a booking, be sure to know where you are staying and have a confirmation number for the hotel room, etc. If your agent submits you for a job that you get called in for and you do not feel comfortable doing it, then talk to your agent and don't go on the casting. Communication is key for everyone.

My child is 12 years old. How do I know that the people she is working with are safe?

All parents are concerned with this and should be. It will be comforting to know that you (the parent) will always be on the set with your child until they reach the age of majority at 18 years old. Legitimate agents are licensed in their state. If they receive complaints, they may lose their license. So, rest assured that agencies that are established and have been in business for some time are safe.

The agent receives breakdowns from breakdown services which they pay to receive. Only agents and casting directors get these breakdowns. The casting directors who call the talent in for an audition are working on behalf of their client who has hired them to find the right talent for the job.

Example: Let's say that the client is Target. Target hires a casting director to hold an audition for their photo shoot. The casting director puts out the audition notice on the breakdowns. Your child's agent sees the job on the breakdowns and submits your child for the job. From the submission, your child is chosen to audition. The date and time of the audition will be given to you by your agent. Then you go to the casting. If the client chooses your child to do the job, then you will be given the date and time of the shoot. All parties involved are professionals and you (the parent) are always present with your child, so everything should be safe. However, if you notice anything that is not right or that your child is not being treated properly, then you pick up the phone and call your agent immediately. If your child is shooting a commercial, TV show or film and they are with the SAG/AFTRA union, then all non-safety issues should be reported to SAG/AFTRA. Your union protects you from any problem that occurs on the set.

CHAPTER 7

PAGEANTRY TRAINING

Do you recommend to young girls who are interested in becoming a model that they should get involved in pageants?

I fully support that the more experience a young model acquires on stage, the better. Pageantry affords this experience.

PAGEANTRY TRAINING ──────────────

I have trained several girls to prepare for pageants. Some of the models that I have trained have done both modeling and pageantry. The pageantry training has become closer to the way a model walks in recent years. The biggest difference between pageants versus fashion shows is that there is rarely a long runway for pageants. Pageantry walks are more structured as well. Their posture and the way they carry themselves is similar to a model, but still different. A runway model has more movement in their hip area and the walk is a bit more relaxed in style.

I trained a girl for the Miss USA Pageant and she placed in the top five. I also trained my daughter for the Miss Hawaiian Tropic Pageant and she won the regional division and went on to the State Pageant. I have also worked to train girls for the Little Miss Teen, Miss and Mrs. Santa Clarita Valley Pageant in California, under its director Miss Mardi Rivetti.

Pageants are a great way to work on your overall confidence. The speaking component is a part of most of the pageants. Communication is key in the entertainment industry and modeling industry. People like to work with models that are fun and have good personalities.

I was asked a few years back to write an article in *Pageantry Magazine*. The article was titled "It's All in the Packaging," and can be found in Chapter 12, "Breaking Into The Business – Articles."

Suzanne Speaks

Most pageant contestants hire a professional, like me, to help them with their walk and prepare them for the speech component. It is not mandatory, but if you are wanting to be a serious contender, training is important.

TIPS

Pageantry training is a fabulous way to learn and build one's confidence.

The pageants that are run well usually have training workshops as well as some etiquette training.

Being part of a pageant is a good way to gain more experience and stage presence.

It's always important to build your resume, and adding pageantry is a plus.

Q & A

What do you wear on stage when you do a pageant?

Pageants usually have 3 categories

1. Business Attire

2. Swimsuit

3. Evening Gown

Who pays for the training for the pageant?

The pageant provides a workshop, but their training is minimal. Most pageant contestants hire a professional to train them. This is paid for by the contestant or by the contestant's sponsors.

Do you have to buy the clothing you wear in the pageants?

Usually, yes – especially in the smaller pageants. If you are in the Miss USA or Miss America Pageant, they may have a vendor supply the bathing suits for the contestants.

What is the speech component like?

Some pageants will have "pop" questions that they ask. These questions usually relate to world affairs. So, the contestants have to be up on what is going on in the world and share their opinion in their answer. Some pageants will have their contestants speak about their sponsor.

How do I qualify to be in a pageant?

Every pageant has a Pageant Director. Some pageants accept anyone who registers for their pageant. Others will hold an open call for those that are interested in being in their pageant and then choose a certain number of contestants per age category, as they have limited space.

How tall do I have to be to be in a pageant?

There is no height requirement to be in a pageant.

What do you win in a pageant?

If you win or place in a regional pageant, you are usually given a trophy. Some pageants give scholarships toward furthering education and some pageants offer cash prizes. When you enter a pageant it is good to check their standing on awards.

How do I qualify for the bigger pageants like Miss California or other state pageants that lead to Miss American and Miss USA?

Before you can enter to be in a large state pageant, you must have been in at least one regional pageant that you placed. If you win in a state pageant, then you qualify to move on to Miss America or Miss USA.

How do I get rid of stage fright if I have to speak on stage?

The more you put yourself out there by getting up in front of people to talk or perform, the better. You gain confidence by doing. I suggest that you get involved in school plays and take acting classes, where it is part of the curriculum to get up on stage in front of people. Practice makes perfect and diminishes fear.

Should I be in a pageant even if I don't think that I would win because of the competition?

You should never enter a competition with only winning in mind. You enter these types of things for growth and personal development. The training is helpful for anything that you do in life. Many long-lasting friendships are gained by being a part of pageant competitions or even model conventions. It is always about each individual's experience and development. If you win it is an added plus.

CHAPTER 8

BLAM GLAM

What are the things that models need for their business?

As a model, YOU are your business. You are the package that you are selling. It is important to look like a model from head to toe. Your skin, makeup, teeth, hair, nails, toenails, body and wardrobe have to be in extra tip top shape. If you do not look your best, you will not book the job. Attention has to be focused on YOU. Be sure to bring a good attitude and a happy personality with you as well.

SKIN

An important part of a model's asset is her SKIN. How many models do you see in magazines with broken out, scarred or uneven skin? Yes, makeup does help, but for the most part a model's skin is toned, clean and smooth.

Your skin and complexion must be next-to-perfection, free of pimples, brown spots, blackheads or whiteheads. When you are a teenager, you go through many changes and your skin is one of the things that does change drastically throughout the teenage years. If you are having difficulty with your skin, I recommend that you go to a dermatologist. This way they can help you with topicals that can calm your skin down.

Skin Types at a Glance

Your skin type is determined by how much, or how little, oil your skin produces. Genes, diet, stress level, medication, and skincare regimen will help determine this also.

OILY SKIN: Shiny skin, enlarged pores, prone to blackheads and blemishes, some tightness.

COMBINATION / NORMAL: Medium pores, smooth and even texture, good circulation, healthy color, may tend toward dryness on the cheeks, may be oily in the T-zone.

SENSITIVE: Thin, delicate, fine pores. Flushes easily, prone to broken capillaries, frequently allergic, can be rashy.

DRY: Feels tight, especially after cleansing; fine wrinkles, flaking, red patches. In women of color, appears ashy or dull from dead skin buildup.

AGING OR SUN DAMAGED: Feels tight, visible wrinkles, slack skin tone – especially around cheeks and jawline – leathery texture, broken capillaries.

BASIC 5 STEP REGIMEN ——————————

Step 1: Cleanse

Use a cleanser that is appropriate for your skin type. Use an emollient cleanser (cleanser that is milky or creamy) for normal or dry skin. For oily skin use more of a gel-type cleanser or an oil-free cleanser for very oily skin.

Massage cleanser around your face in circular motions. Rinse well with warm water that is not too cold or too hot.

Dermatological surgeon, Barney Kenet, says one of the biggest mistakes that Americans make is over-washing their face. Washing too often and too aggressively can strip skin of surface lipids. This will cause skin to lose its natural protection and become dry and irritated (even with oily skin.)

Step 2: Exfoliate / Mask

Approximately every 3 weeks, new cells push up from the lowest layer of the epidermis and move toward the surface. Exfoliation helps shed the skin of the old skin cells to promote a healthy skin glow.

Rub a bit of scrub between the palms of the hand and massage gently onto the face. Again, don't scrub too hard! And never use a loofah on the face. To get your circulation going, splash with cool water.

Exfoliate about 2-3 times a week.

Mask – Depending on your skin type, a mask can be used about once a week to deep clean pores. Gently apply a mask to entire face, avoiding the eyes and under the eye area. Relax and let dry for 10-15 minutes being careful not to "crack" your mask. Soften with warm water and gently remove mask. Pat your skin dry.

Step 3: Toner

Do not use a toner that contains alcohol (this will do more harm than good). Alcohol-free toners will create the "shrunken pores" effect and cut through the oil without the drying astringent properties.

Apply toner to a cotton ball and swipe over face. Again, avoid the eye and under-eye area.

In the heat of the summer, stash your toner in the fridge. The cold toner will feel good on the skin and help it look firmer.

Step 4: Moisturize / Protect

Everyone should moisturize! Moisturizers soften skin, bind water to the skin, plump up skin cells, and create a barrier between the skin and the atmosphere. Use a heavier moisturizer or cream for dry skin, or a light lotion for oily skin.

Apply a dime-size dab to the palm of your hands and rub hands together. Then use an upward, circular motion to lightly massage moisturizer into your skin.

Step 5: Eye Cream

Gently pat the eye cream under your eye with fourth finger (the weakest) starting at the outer corner and working inward.

Don't over-moisturize! More is not better. Too much moisturizer can lead to clogged pores and blackheads.

MAKEUP

It is important that the model shows up to auditions with her makeup on. If you are 14 years old and up, you should be wearing makeup to enhance your look. If you are under 14, I suggest that you wear minimal makeup to your castings.

To learn how to do your makeup, I suggest that you go to Sephora or a department store and have a makeup artist at the store apply your makeup. It is usually complimentary, and you will learn a lot by watching. It can be overwhelming to go into a makeup store and know exactly what shade of makeup to use as a base, blush, etc.

HAIR

It is important to choose a hair style that looks good on you and compliments the shape of your face. Healthy looking hair is an asset to any model. Find a shampoo and conditioner that works on your hair without weighing it down.

BIKINI READY

If there are bathing suits in a Fashion Show, the client may ask for you to come bikini ready. This means that you should have taken the proper steps to be sure that you have shaved your legs and done proper grooming to wear a bathing suit on the runway or in a photo shoot. You may also want to use some self-tanner.

NAILS

Your hands and your nails are seen in photos. It is important that your hands and your nails are always in tip top shape. Many people in the industry want your nails to look natural. The length of the nail should not be too long. It is fine to have acrylic nails, but again, not too long.

THE MANICURE ———————————————————

Step 1: Remove any old polish with 100% cotton balls. Use a cotton swab (such as Q-tip) to remove stubborn polish on cuticles.

Step 2: File and shape your nails in one direction only. Filing back and forth can cause splitting and cracking. Use a soft grade file.

Step 3: Massage a light cuticle oil or moisturizer into the nail and cuticle area for a minute or two. Then, soak fingers in warm soapy water for about five minutes to soften the cuticles. A great inexpensive oil to use is vegetable cooking oil from the kitchen.

Step 4: Gently push cuticles back with the tip of an orangewood stick.

Step 5: Rub your hands with moisturizer. Then wipe your nails with a clean cloth to get rid of residual oils on the nail and get ready for the polish.

Step 6: Apply a base coat to help the polish adhere. Then apply your polish. One coat is fine, but if you apply more, make sure to let each coat dry for a few minutes in between to prevent creasing.

Step 7: If you're in a hurry, apply a fast-drying topcoat. The only drawback is that the topcoat makes the top layer of polish feel dry to the touch, but the polish will still "dent" from wet polish underneath.

Daily Regimen

1. Cleanse and wash hands.

2. Moisturize – twice a day preferably.

3. Use sunscreen – exposure to the sun can accelerate aging and brown spots.

4. Wear gloves when working with harsh detergents or chemicals.

Tips for Extra Moisturizing for Hands and Feet

Use a heavy moisturizer, Bag Balm or wheat germ oil on hands and feet before bed. Cover hands with cotton gloves and feet with socks. Both will be super soft in the morning.

THE PEDICURE

Step 1: Remove old polish with cotton and clip toenails straight across using nail clippers. Shape and smooth with nail file, filing in one direction only.

Step 2: Fill a basin with warm water and bath salts, kosher salt, or Epsom salts and a few drops of your favorite essential oil or bath oil. Soak your feet for 8 to 10 minutes.

Step 3: Apply an exfoliating body scrub or foot sloughing cream to a loofah or wet pumice stone, and scrub rough patches on the balls and heels of the feet. Use a nailbrush to scrub around and under the toenails. Rinse your feet.

Step 4: Massage your feet with moisturizer or cuticle oil and use an orangewood stick to gently push back the cuticles and dry skin. Trim any hangnails with a clipper.

Step 5: Wash and dry nail area to free it of leftover moisturizer. Separate toes with a foam separator or paper towel. Apply base coat, then polish. Let dry for 5 minutes.

 # *Suzanne Speaks*

As a model, all attention is on YOU! You must be in tip top shape, from clear skin, healthy hair, pretty nails, and makeup that enhances your features.

TIPS

- Do not pick at your skin. When you pick at your skin or press hard to try to pop a pimple, you can actually damage the delicate skin on your face and cause scarring.

- Giving yourself a facial or going to a professional for a facial once a month is a good idea.

- It is important to have a good skincare regime and stick to it. There are some good ones that you can try like Arbonne, Rodan and Fields, or Clarisma found in Ulta. Or, you can try over the counter cosmetic lines that are sold in department stores.

- Cetaphil is a very gentle cleanser that can be used and is sold at CVS and Walgreens.

- Invest in a good pair of sunglasses so you stop squinting when you are outdoors. Squinting causes lines between your eyebrows. Also, cataracts in eyes are a result of not wearing sunglasses when young. Cataracts show up later in life.

- Zit Blitz – mix 1 tablespoon of apple cider vinegar or white vinegar into a cup of warm water and then pat on face with cotton balls. Applied once a week, it will keep pimples at bay because the bacteria that cause pimples is not acid-tolerant, and will die.
  *from Tammy Ha, cosmetic chemist formerly with Neutrogena.

- Always wear sunblock every day, even in winter.

- Remember that makeup is used to enhance your features. Do not overdo the makeup and look like you are painted.

- When you are booked for a job, there is usually a makeup and hair stylist at the booking.

- If you are doing a fashion show at a department store, they will ask you to come hair and makeup ready. So, it is necessary that you know how to do your own makeup and that you bring your makeup bag with you.

- For long hair, be sure to have a health-trim every six to eight weeks to keep from getting split ends.

- Watch out for too hot a curling iron or straightening iron. Use product that can protect your hair from the excess heat, so you don't fry your hair.

- I use L'Oreal Sublime Bronze Self-Tanning Towelettes for my self-tan. They are easy to use, and the tan looks so natural.

- Be sure that you carry your own razor in your model bag just in case you need a touch up. Never use another person's razor.

- Always ask when you are booked for a job what color the client would prefer on your nails.

- Some photo shoots have a manicurist on the set; however, this is not the norm.

- Well-manicured toes are a must in case you wear open toed shoes in the photo shoot.

- If you are booked for a Runway Fashion Show, it is best for your nails to be either done in a French manicure or a light color.

- Daily skincare is very important. Developing good habits early on will reward you later in adult life.

Q & A

How old should a model be when they start a skincare routine?

At 10 years old, start cleansing your face with Cetaphil, which you can pick up at most drugstores. By the age of thirteen, it's recommended that you start a skincare routine, which includes cleansing and moisturizing twice a day. It is also important to use a sunscreen daily. During the teenage years, many teens experience skin issues, sensitivity or breakouts. There are many product lines that deal with these issues. However, I recommend a visit to a Dermatologist who can lead you in the right direction for proper treatment.

Do I have to get a professional mani/pedi?

Although it is so nice to pamper yourself and have a professional mani/pedi, it is not necessary. You can go to a beauty supply or drugstore to buy the supplies you need to do your own mani/pedi at home.

Should I get acrylic or gel nails?

If you choose to get acrylic nails, there is upkeep and expense with them. Every 7-10 days you will need to have a fill. Also, as a model, you do not want your nails to be too long. If you do get acrylics, then be sure to make them look natural. For acrylics, I would suggest that you go to a professional.

Gel nails are similar to acrylics but do less damage to your own nail. Gel nails help to strengthen your own nails, but do not extend the nail to look longer. Acrylics are used to make your nails stronger and longer.

At what age do I need to groom my eyebrows?

There are several ways to groom your eyebrows.
1. Tweeze (with tweezers)
2. Wax
3. Thread

I have done all three of these. The one I like the best is threading. You need to find a good qualified aesthetician to do it for you. I have waxed, but I have had some of my skin taken off because the wax was either too hot or my skin was too sensitive in that area. Tweezing is good to do in-between your threading appointments. Threading is also very good to do on your upper lip.

Once I start modeling, do I need to get facials?

It is important that your skin is always in its best condition once you begin modeling. In the teen years, it may be best to go to a Dermatologist to take care of your skin if you have breakouts or sensitivity. In your 20s and 30s, I suggest professional facials so that you always keep your skin looking fabulous. However, if you cannot afford this, then go to Sephora or Ulta to find a skincare system that is right for your skin type that you can use at home.

Is it OK if I color my own hair?

Please do not color your own hair! In fact, most clients are looking for models who have natural healthy-looking hair. Over-processed hair is not pretty or fresh looking. If you are a dark blonde, some highlights may work without looking fake. Fake looking hair is not what the industry is looking for. Natural beauty is what the client likes best.

BOTOX / FILLERS

What are your thoughts regarding Botox and other injectables for models?

If you are younger than 30 years old, you should not need to use injectables or Botox. There shouldn't be a need for them because you are young. Most agencies frown on models getting their lips blown up and looking unnatural. Breast implants are also frowned upon by agents today. Even too much unnatural hair color is frowned upon.

Agents are looking for naturally attractive models. Now having said that, models that are still working in the industry in there 40s – 60s may want to use Botox and some fillers.

Tip: Be careful when you do use Botox and fillers, that you go to someone who is well trained and who doesn't overdo it. You still need to look natural; duck lips can put you out of business really quick!

CHAPTER 9

TOOLS OF THE MODELING TRADE

What are the tools of the trade that I need to be a professional model?

In every profession, there are tools and skills that are needed for you to perform your job. In the modeling business, as soon as you complete a job or booking, you are looking for the next opportunity. One thing you must have is a tough skin. Rejection is part of this business.

BUSINESS CARD

I have always carried business cards with me at all times. You never know who you are going to meet or where you might meet them. An 8x10 headshot or a zed card are too big to carry around in your everyday life. But a business card is not. A professional business card for the entertainment industry should have your photo on it along with your social media contacts and your email. A telephone number is optional.

TEST SHOOTS WITH PHOTOGRAPHERS

Test shoots are photo shoots that you do with a photographer to build your portfolio. In the beginning when you start out as a model and have not booked any jobs yet, you need to have photos for your portfolio for clients to see how you photograph. By doing test shoots you gain experience as well as photos for your portfolio. Test shoots are usually done in a barter type situation. The photographer wants to experiment with lighting or a new lens and the model needs photos, so they collaborate together. This works out great for both the photographer and the model.

PHOTOS, ZED CARD, PORTFOLIO

Additional info in Chapter 5

PHOTOS

Photos are the most important tool that a model can have. Photos are sent electronically by your agent to casting. If your photos are not up to par, you will not get called in for the audition.

Photos in your portfolio are important as well. When you go to a casting for a print job, the client will ask to see your portfolio. If you have tear sheets in your portfolio it is a plus. Work begets work. Clients feel more comfortable when they see that other clients have invested their money in you by hiring you to do their advertising campaign. If you are just starting out and you do not yet have tear sheets in your portfolio, then ten great photos of you from various photo shoots will be a good start.

An 8x10 photo is a headshot of you with your resume attached to the back of the photo. Your 8x10 photo is usually used for acting.

ZED CARD

The zed card for a model is equivalent to a sampling of your portfolio. It is a selection of photos that are produced into a card that the model leaves with the client at an audition. This card has a headshot on the front and 4 photos on the back. When you put a zed card together, you as the model must decide how to package yourself. That will determine the type of photos and clothing you will choose to accent your strength as a model in your photo shoot.

PORTFOLIO

A portfolio is a book that is filled with acetate sheets for you to put photos and tear sheets to be displayed. When you go on auditions for print jobs, you take your portfolio with you so that you can let the client view your work. Your photos also allow the client to see how you photograph.

With the technology of today's world, many models will upload their photos on their iPad for clients to view instead of using a portfolio. It is less expensive to use an iPad, because you do not have to print the photos for your portfolio. However, there are mixed reviews about using an iPad versus a portfolio. It is best that once you are signed with an agent, that you check to see what your agent prefers. Every region and market will be different regarding this choice.

LA CASTING

Once you are signed with an agent, your photos will be put on the LA Casting site for submissions. LA Casting – Casting Networks is the leading provider of casting and audition management software. There are 23,000 industry professionals who use Casting Networks to facilitate over a million auditions per year.

REPRESENTATION / AGENT

It is important for every model to be represented by an agent. A good agent will submit you for jobs that are right for you so you can have the opportunity to audition for the job and secure a booking.

MODEL BAG FOR FEMALE MODELS ————————

Every model needs a model bag. It's a tote bag that the model carries with the things she needs when going to a booking or an audition.

- Nail File
- Hairbrush/Comb
- Deodorant
- Toothbrush/Mouthwash
- Makeup Bag
- Personal Razor
- Hair Spray (if you use it)
- Lint Roller
- Strapless Bra Nude
- Pasties
- Nude G-string/Extra Panties
- Body Slimmer
- Selection of Shoes & High Heels
- Small Selection of Earrings (for Runway Show)
- Dress Shields
- Scarf or Face Shield for Changing (to avoid getting makeup on clothing)
- Wash Cloth
- Hair Pins (to put hair up if asked)
- Visine Eye Drops

- For print and runway audition you may be asked to try on clothing, so it is best to be prepared with the proper undergarments.

- Dress Shields – use maxi pads with the adhesive wings for sticking.

- You should have a pair of heels with you at every audition. For a runway audition it is a must to be wearing a heel for your walking audition. If you want, you can put your heels on in the car just before you go into your audition.

MODEL BAG FOR MALE MODELS ——————

The male model will need to carry the following in their model bag.

- Deodorant
- Makeup Base (that matches and blends into your skin color)
- Razor
- Electric Razor (in case your beard gets a 5 o'clock shadow)
- Toothbrush/Mouthwash
- Plain White Crew Neck T-Shirt
- Black Dress Socks
- Chapstick
- Nail File (and clean nails)
- Book (to read on set)
- Snacks and Water
- Visine Eye Drops

SHOES FOR RUNWAY – WOMEN ——————

Spring Shoes
Strappy Heels – Black & Tan
Sandals – Flat & Strappy
Tennis Shoes – White

Winter
Pumps – Black & Nude
Evening – Gold & Silver
Boots – Black & Brown

SHOES FOR RUNWAY – MEN ——————

Black Dress Shoe
Brown Dress Shoe
Vans

WEBSITE

Should a model have their own website? In today's world, the more you have on the internet that is readily accessible, the better. Actors, models and singers have their own websites.

With kids under 18 years old, I would be very careful about websites. They can have them, but it is imperative that the parent manage everything that goes on with their website. The website can be used to upload pictures as well as fashion show videos that they have participated in.

SOCIAL MEDIA (Goal 10,000 Followers)

How Models Generate Momentum to Get More Work

Social Media: Social media has become a key factor in gaining more work as a model. The more followers you have on Instagram, the better. Some of the top agencies will not even accept a model unless they have at least 10,000 followers.

- Think of creative ways to post pictures of yourself looking like a model on Instagram. Get all dressed up and do your hair in different ways, and have a friend take photos of you and post every day.

- Go to a store and choose a few looks and then go to the dressing room and try them on. Have a friend snap a photo of you in the dressing room with that look and post it on Instagram.

- If you go to a casting, do a runway show or a photo shoot, be sure to take behind the scene photos. Post the photo so your followers will see that you are actively pursuing your career.

MODEL VOCABULARY

PORTFOLIO: Contains professional photographs and tear sheets that show client examples of your work.

ZED CARD / COMP CARD: A group of pictures showing a model in different poses and with different "looks." Normally the front will have a headshot and the back of the card will contain 3-4 other photos. The model's name, agency and statistics are listed on the card.

TEAR SHEETS: These are pages from magazines and other publications that show a model at work. Since tear sheets indicate experience, they are essential credentials.

TESTING: Testing is the term used for a photographic session to produce pictures for your portfolio and composite.

GO-SEES / AUDITION / INTERVIEW: A job interview with a photographer or a client.

CASTING: A casting is an interview for a television commercial.

CALLBACK: This is a second audition for a job.

HEADSHOT: A closeup photograph of a model's head and face.

A SHOOT: Time spent in a studio or on location with a photographer or camera crew for an assignment.

ON LOCATION: This is where the shoot takes place. It can be a place you know well or an exotic spot on the other side of the world. If you are working for a client, this is your opportunity to travel, with all expenses paid including your model fee.

VOUCHER / INVOICE: A voucher or invoice is a payment contract between you and the client. It is essential that you fill these out correctly with all information printed neatly. You give the client a copy, your agency a copy, and retain a copy for your records. Never allow a photographer or client add any conditions to the voucher or delete and reference to reproduction rights. Always call the agency if you have any questions.

Suzanne Speaks

Models should not limit themselves to just runway and print modeling. It is important to be well-rounded and learn to act in commercials as well as take an acting class for TV/film. Many times, when a company is doing an advertising campaign, they choose to have the same model do both the print and commercial for the campaign. You must know how to move in front of the camera for the print portion of the campaign and also know how to deliver a commercial for the television advertising part of the campaign.

TIPS

⌐ I recommend taking a hosting class as many models transition into this type of work as well. Tyra Banks and Heidi Klum are examples of models who parlayed their modeling careers into television shows, Tyra Banks/America's Next Top Model and Heidi Klum/Project Runway.

⌐ To keep your model bag organized, be sure that you carry your makeup in a zippered cosmetic bag.

⌐ Find a trendy smart-looking model bag to carry that matches your signature style.

⌐ Be sure to use a spray cleaner on your makeup brushes after each use. Another way to clean brushes is to shampoo them once a month.

⌐ Stay current with your photos, especially if you change your look.

⌐ Many of the models I have worked with who have built up an Instagram following have been pursued by clothing brands to become one of their brand ambassadors. They send them clothing to wear for free as long as they post photos of themselves wearing their clothing on their Instagram.

Q & A

What is a Work Permit?

A valid work permit is usually required when your child (under 18) works. The regulations regarding work permits vary from state to state and city to city. Your agent may have a copy of a work permit to give to you. If not, to obtain one in your area, call the State Labor Commissioner, Department of Labor or Local School Superintendent's office. This permit will need to be signed by your child's principal to take them out of school for work. Your child must maintain a required grade average. If they fall behind, the principal can revoke the work permit until a better grade average is obtained.

What is a Coogan Account?

This is a special bank account that is required for a parent to set up for their child who is under the age of 18. A Coogan Account insures that child actors, models and athletes (and other young performers) receive this portion of their earnings when they reach majority age of 18. January 1, 2000, changes in California law affirmed that earnings by minors in the entertainment industry are the property of the minor and not their parents; this change in California law requires that 15% of all minor's earnings must be set aside in a blocked trust account commonly known as a Coogan Account.

Is there a union for models?

No, there is not a union for models. The hourly rates are determined by the agents in the city that your agent works. In NYC, the rates are much higher than the rates in California. In NYC, they often have a two-hour minimum rate as well. That is not the case in California or other regional markets. Some models who are "stars" have higher rates than other models.

How do you get training to help you improve and get noticed in the industry?

If you need more runway or print training to work in front of the camera, your agent will suggest a coach. I work with most of the agencies in LA. When they have girls that need training for runway, they call me. I have packaged many models. I have trained them to walk and I produced their zed cards. Then I walk them into agencies to be seen for representation. Agents in LA always welcome a call from me if I have a new model that I have trained. It saves the agent a lot of time, as the model is ready to audition and work.

CHAPTER 10

HEALTH AND FITNESS

How do I know if I am as fit as I need to be, to be a model?

All models must be in shape and keep their body at a proper weight and look toned. After all, YOU are the product that you are selling.

VITAMINS

There is a bewildering array of supplements on pharmacy and grocery store shelves, but you don't have to feel like you're gambling when making your selection. If you decide to enhance your nutrient intake with supplements, look for a vitamin that contains approximately 100% of the recommended daily value or most nutrients. Beyond that, here's what you need to know.

Don't count on a multivitamin's calcium. This nutrient is too bulky to fit 100% of your needs in a simple tablet, so you may need to take a separate supplement. Look for 500 mg to 600 mg tablets of calcium citrate, calcium carbonate or calcium with magnesium or vitamin D.

Consider chewables. If you don't like to swallow pills, a chewable vitamin may give you almost the full amount you need as an adult. If you are under 18, consult your pediatrician for proper dosage and recommendations.

Give your stomach time to adjust. If a multivitamin upsets your stomach, experiment with different brands to see which agrees with you. Give your body a couple of weeks to acclimate to each new brand. Or, try splitting a hefty tablet in half and taking each portion at different times during the day.

Vitamins:

A Essential for good vision, healthy skin, hair, teeth and bones; can boost immunity and help protect against cancer.

B3 Niacin helps your body convert food into energy and promotes normal appetite, digestion and nerve functions; in high amounts, can lower cholesterol.

B6 Promotes the body's use of protein to make cells, helps produce hemoglobin, insulin and antibodies to fight infection, can reduce PMS symptoms, may protect against heart disease and stroke.

B12 Builds genetic material needed by cells, helps create red blood cells, helps your body use fatty acids, may protect memory and cognitive function.

Folic Acid Prevents neural tube defects during pregnancy, helps produce

DNA and RNA for new cells, helps prevent heart disease and cancer.

C Promotes wound healing, healthy gums, proper immune function and collagen formation, helps prevent heart disease and cancer.

D3 Maintains healthy bones by boosting calcium absorption, promotes good immune system function, may reduce risk of colon cancer; 5,000 IU daily.

E Strengthens the immune system and balances cholesterol, great for the skin and hair; 400 mg daily.

Fish Oil Omega 3 Good for overall health for your body to function well.

EXERCISE

All models must be in shape and keep their body at a proper weight and look toned.

It is important to have scheduled days and times to work out. If you are a disciplined person, then you can do this by yourself and schedule your workouts at least three times a week at a gym. If you are not a disciplined person, then I suggest that you hire a trainer and work out with them three times a week. In some cases, it is a good idea to work out with a trainer in the beginning, to learn what exercises to do to stay in shape and work on problem areas if you have them. Then, try it on your own to see if you can be disciplined enough to keep up the routine workouts on your own.

Be sure that you eat a healthy diet and exercise, so that you maintain your weight. This pertains to the model who is 16 years old and up. There is nothing worse than pigging out on junk food and gaining 5-10 pounds, and then your agent calls you with a request interview for a great opportunity, and you know that you may not fit in the clothing! There is no way that you can lose 5-10 pounds in one or two days. Discipline is key.

Suzanne Speaks

It is important to look your best and feel your best. It is also important to have a sound body, spirit and mind. To acquire health, it is up to you to educate yourself on how to keep yourself feeling great and looking great. Most models, both male and female, spend a lot of time researching how to do this. From taking the proper vitamins to working out and maintaining a healthy lifestyle. Many models work with trainers. YOU are the total package that you are selling, so you want to package yourself in the best way possible. It's not enough these days to just be pretty or good looking.

TIPS

Discipline is the key to sustaining a healthy lifestyle.

No one is going to pay you $200.00 an hour if you aren't in tip top condition. Remember, YOU are what the client is buying.

You can't do a runway show or a print job if you are sick. Take your vitamins, get your rest, and eat a balanced diet.

Q & A

Do a lot of models have eating disorders?

In my experience, I have not come across models with eating disorders. I know that there are girls out there that have eating disorders, but I can't say that it's directly related to modeling. It is true that a model has to be a specific size to model and that the look is to be tall and thin, especially for Runway Modeling.

There should be no reason for a model to go up and down in weight if they eat a healthy diet and exercise on a regular basis. This does take discipline. The models that are working models and work all of the time have their diet and exercise regimen down to a science. The way one eats becomes a way of life so that weight gain is not a worry. Healthy eating habits are established when you are young. A lot of sugar and junk food are not only unhealthy for you, but will make you gain weight. If you are a person who cannot stay away from cookies and pastries, you may have a problem with your weight. Eating a lot of this kind of tempting food will defeat the purpose of being at your model weight. Salads, fruits, lean protein and vegetables are the best things for you and will keep your weight where you want it at all times. Also, getting exercise is very important for everyone, not just models. If you have fallen into bad eating habits, it will show on your skin, your energy level, as well as your overall attitude. I suggest that if you are struggling with your weight because of bad eating habits, it is best to go to a nutritionist who can guide you and help you get on the right track in a healthy way.

If I am too muscular and need to lean out a bit, what type of diet do you recommend?

I recommend eating one food group at each meal.

Example:
Morning up until lunch. Eat fruit that is low in sugar (apples, berries, and a scoop of protein powder in a shake)
Lunch. Eat all carbs (pasta, salad, vegetables)
Dinner. Eat all protein (chicken, fish)

*Eating this way allows for easy digestion and you get a balanced meal over the course of the day. Stay away from bread!

CHAPTER 11

FASHION WEEK

Why is Fashion Week such a big deal?

Fashion Week is what the fashionistas of the world run to see!
Designers present their latest collections each year in the spring
and fall in Paris, Milan, London, NYC, Los Angeles and other cities
in the US.

FASHION WEEK ───────────────────

Fashion Week is held twice a year, spring and fall in NYC and LA. Designers show their new collections for the year at Fashion Week. Fashion Week is a week-long extravaganza of designers presenting their latest collections which range from sportswear to couture to evening wear. There are several platforms of shows that take place in both cities during Fashion Week. The designers vie for a spot on the runway for the best time slot to feature their collection.

A casting is held a week or so prior to Fashion Week for the models. The designers or their assistants are at the casting, along with the show producers, to make their selection of the models they want in their show.

Most of the models in LA do not get paid to do Fashion Week shows. They do it for exposure. Models who are just starting out in the business do it for the experience. In NYC some of the shows for Fashion Week are paid, but many are not.

When I was modeling in NYC and LA in the 70s, 80s and 90s, we were always paid. But as time went on, there were so many girls that were not represented by agencies that came to castings. These girls were willing to work for free with hopes of being discovered. This hurt the business and the models represented by agencies. However, there are many other runway shows throughout the year that are booked through the agencies and are paid. Fashion Week is an exception.

Suzanne Speaks

If you are a new model who has trained with someone and know how to walk, it is a fabulous opportunity for a new model to do Fashion Week even though you are not paid. It's a win-win for a new model. You meet designers, gain experience, exposure, and you can network – meeting people in the industry.

For Fashion Week, the model will be required to be at the location very early in the afternoon for hair and makeup and to try on the clothing. The shows are late afternoon into the evening. It is up to you as a model to know when Fashion Week takes place in your city. Some models who live in LA will travel to NYC for NY Fashion Week and other markets, and then come back to LA to do LA Fashion Week.

TIPS

- I always have new models that I train audition for Fashion Week in LA to gain experience. NYC also has Fashion Week, and in Miami there is Swim Fashion Week.

- There are Fashion Weeks in many cities across the United States. Check your local area and look into how you might become a part of them.

- Be prepared for things to run late. If your show is to go on at 8:00 pm, it may run an hour or more late.

- Bring food and water with you for the day.

- Bring a book with you as you may have a lot of waiting around before the show begins.

- Ask for business cards of everyone you meet, including the hair stylist and makeup artist. Begin to collect these cards, as these are all contacts that you may be able to use in the future.

🔖 Try to get the business cards from all of the photographers that are present. Tell them that you are interested in purchasing the runway shots that they get of you on the runway when you walk. These photos can be used on your next zed card or in your portfolio to show that you have worked.

🔖 You should have your own business card with your photo on it to give to contacts that you meet as well. Your zed card may be given out, but it is usually not necessary for a zed card to be given to everyone you meet. A business card will suffice in many situations.

Q & A

What does Fashion Week look like?

Fashion Week is usually very crazy, and a lot is packed into a week's time. When you audition for Fashion Week, there will be a line of models waiting to be seen. It is usually held in a big room and there is no music to walk to. They will have you sign in, then they have several models line up in a straight line and have all of you walk at the same time. There will be a table of people sitting there watching you. These are the designers who are participating in the Fashion Week shows. The designers who like you will ask for your zed card. Sometimes they will ask you to try on one of their garments. Usually if they ask you to try something on, it is a good sign.

Is there a Kid's Fashion Week?

Yes, there are Fashion Weeks for kids. Check out the following platforms: NYC Fashion Week for Kids, Staten Island Fashion Week, Houston Fashion Week, Dallas Fashion Week, Kid's Fashion Week in Orlando Florida, Orlando International Fashion Week.

In NYC and LA, some children's designers will participate in Fashion Week. However, they are mixed in with all designers in participation.

CHAPTER 12

BREAKING INTO THE BUSINESS

What are some of the ways I share my knowledge in the modeling industry?

Besides training young models to be successful in the modeling industry, I have also contributed several articles for various publications, providing tips, information and answering questions I am frequently asked.

PUBLISHED ARTICLES ─────────────

Formula for Success

By Suzanne Von Schaack
Actress/Model/Guest Instructor

How can I be successful in the business? This question has been asked over and over by the students that I teach. The answer... success is where preparation meets opportunity. So prepare, prepare, prepare!

Going to class isn't the only thing you need to do to be professional. It's the entire package that an agent or casting director is interested in. You are the product that you are selling. Your look (your style), personality, your attitude, makeup, clothes, nails, confidence, body (measurements), all of these things come into play when you are preparing to compete as a professional.

If you need to knock off a few pounds, buff up, color your hair, be more friendly or assertive, or maybe project a different style in photos – it's all up to you to seek out the professionals who can help you to create your image and at the same time be diligent about your training. After putting your entire package together, "you" then take yourself and your talent and put yourself in a place where your preparation can meet opportunity.

A model convention is a great place to start and afford you many great opportunities. Seeking an agent is a move forward too. Don't forget – do everything you can to be fully prepared. Good luck!

Preparation + Opportunity = Success

Follow Through

By Suzanne Von Schaack
Professional Model & Runway Coach

The lack of follow through is the downfall of many industry professionals. Cards are passed, numbers are exchanged and telephone calls are made, yet nothing happens. Why? Why did I get through the door and yet did not get a callback? Why did I get a callback and yet I didn't get signed? The answer is "communication."

Not only is making a good first impression based on a well-groomed professional but also on personality, style and communication skills. The art of communication is accomplished in several ways: voice, diction, charm, personality, body language, persuasion, enthusiasm and listening. All of which are projected over and through the words spoken and the spirit of an individual's persona. You must sound the way you look and look the way you sound.

In our business, "image" is everything. However, this is not limited to how you dress, use makeup or your manicure. No! Image is also about your voice, diction, vocabulary, handshake, and formulation of ideas and even decision making.

Use every aspect of "you" to make a lasting impression. Make the best of who you are in all aspects and in the presentation of yourself. Most of all... follow through.

It's all in the Packaging – Pageantry Magazine
By Suzanne Von Schaack

Seeking success as a performer or model isn't easy, right? This international runway model and actress knows just how you feel – and she's grateful to teach you her success secrets.

I truly believe that talent always surfaces; but it is up to you to showcase yourself in the proper arena to be recognized by those who can help you achieve your goals and dreams. As talent, you must understand that this business called "show business" is not any different than any other business. However, in this case, you are the product that is being "sold" or "bought," then "packaged" for use in a film, print advertisement, commercial, or fashion magazine layout.

The trick is to become the person whom the people who do the packaging choose to use in their projects. There are several ingredients that help to make this happen: training, image, connections, networking, marketability, and talent. I believe in the adage that "image is everything." Image does not have to mean gorgeous, but it does require that you project the look or style that could be marketed for particular projects.

I remember going on a big audition for a new Black Velvet liquor ad campaign. The advertising agency was looking for a new girl to sign a contract for two years. She had to be blonde and she had to wear a slinky black velvet evening dress and look sultry. I showed up at the audition, had my Polaroid taken and the photo attached to my size card, and waited my turn. As I looked the competition over, I thought, we all look like carbon copies of one another.

But as I waited my turn, I heard "oohs" and "aahs" from the photographer and ad agency representatives and clients as they looked at the portfolios of the women who preceded me. They all had numerous published pictures (tear sheets) in their portfolios, while I had only a few test shots and one or two tear sheets in mine. I looked the part. I dressed the part. But... I didn't have the credibility that the others were able to convey. Their portfolios showed more experience by being published in European magazines and print advertisements. They were not any better than me, but they had gone the extra mile to market themselves.

The truth is that in each city in Europe, there are 40 or more magazines to work for, and many more advertisements than here in the United States. Thus, the images of women who had taken advantage of those opportunities shone bigger and brighter than mine. That experience taught me an important lesson. I was on a plane to Europe immediately, and I returned with a portfolio of published work that allowed me to compete for and win modeling jobs here in the US. I never looked back. But the moral of the modeling career story remains as relevant today. Go to Europe or Japan to gain the experience, then get your portfolio together and polish the image you will need to make it once you're back in America.

To prepare for your big opportunities, you must define your type, and then begin to project that image in your personal style, your photographs, the way you sound, as well as in your dress and attitude. There is a look, sound, and feel that each of us projects – a certain quality that makes us unique. In all walks of life, you are selling your image – work with what you've got. If you are a "tough guy," be it, sound it, look it. That goes for models as well as actors – play your role to the hilt.

You must look the way you sound and sound the way you look. For example, if you are a very beautiful girl and you sound like a Valley Girl, or you're a gorgeous guy who sounds like one of TV's Soprano's henchman, well, you may need to work on your voice so that your speech matches your looks. I have often heard agents say, "I met the most gorgeous girl with all the right qualities to be a super model, but when I spoke with her, all I kept thinking was, 'She could be great as long as I can keep her from talking.' So, I passed."

Of course, along with adopting the role that best suits your natural attributes and talents, you also need to study and hone your skills – be it through private lessons from experienced professionals in modeling and talent schools; auditioning for community fashion or entertainment productions; attending workshops; train with known luminaries in the business; or gaining acceptance to public and private universities with colleges in the performing arts. Keep your photo portfolio up-to-date and be sure to find suitable representation for your level of professionalism. Many times, an agent or manager will work successfully for you for a period of time, and then your career might stall. Chances are, you have to change agents in order to move on. Keep your networking options open, so the next move will seem inevitable.

I have found that over the past 30 plus years, I have re-invented myself and reworked my image several times over. I began as a high-fashion model, worked as a catalog model, and as I grew older, became a lifestyle model. Having always worked as a runway model, I decided to broaden my horizons and took acting classes. After two years of studying the Meisner method of acting, I began auditioning and first worked as an extra in the movie "Tootsie" before being upgraded to a role in that film. Encouraged by that success, I went to Los Angeles for TV pilot season, and later moved to Los Angeles permanently.

Modeling jobs came easy to me there, since I had flourished in National and International markets and was by then a big fish in a small pond. The acting, though, was a different story. I still struggle to keep the acting career fires burning. I work, but not as much as I would like to.

Several years ago, I began teaching people interested in modeling and talent careers. My specialty is runway modeling, but I also teach "image" and "personal development." I love helping young people and have mentored some very talented people – many of whom have moved on and are working professionally. Some of them have stayed in touch with me by email or telephone. They are the ones who benefit the most from my lessons. It is important to stay in touch with people who are in a position to help you.

When it comes to networking, it pays to be a self-starter. Work your contacts. Don't wait for your agent or manager to perform for you. They are likely to have many other talents on their roster besides you. Send thank you notes after an audition to the casting director who called you in for the audition. Mail postcards, letting clients and casting agents know of your latest accomplishments. Hand out business cards with your picture on it with a contact number.

By the way, you may notice that all of these promotional ideas project your image. The way in which you pen your thank you notes and the stationary you use, project your image even when your contacts don't physically see you. As I said at the start, "image" is everything. After all is said and done, **my life's work is living the dream and sharing its secrets.**

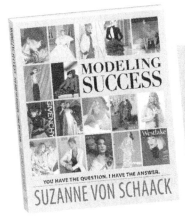

About The Author

Suzanne Von Schaack has worn many different hats within the fashion industry. She has graced the pages of Vogue, Bazaar, L'Official and Cosmopolitan. After meeting Hubert Givenchy at a casting in New York, her life changed. Much of her time after that was spent in Paris walking the runway for the Couture Collections in Paris and Milan, as well as being photographed for the many publications in Paris.

Continuing on a path in the arts, Suzanne studied acting in NYC. Her first movie was *Tootsie*. She then moved to Los Angeles where she continued to work in both the entertainment and modeling business. She has appeared in television series classics such as *Dallas, Dynasty, Ally McBeal, The Young and the Restless*, and was cast in skits for the *Jay Leno Show*. Working in acting roles with Dustin Hoffman, Dabney Coleman, Woody Allen, Fred Williamson, Peter Marshall, Stacy Keach, Gary Busey, Don Wilson and James Franco.

Later, Suzanne fell into the behind the scenes part of the business to wear the hat of *producer*, producing high-end fashion shows for various charity foundations as well as fashion shows for several high school fundraisers. She also produces a show twice a year for iPOP! (International Presentation of Performers). Young talented people attend this convention to be discovered by agents and managers, and to work with professionals in workshops.

Although Suzanne is busy working as a producer, she still keeps active as talent. She recently wrote, produced, and starred in her own short film *The Chains That Bind* (2019). This film is currently making the circuit at film festivals. To date, *The Chains That Bind* has won several awards including: Best Chick Flick, Best Dramedy Short, Semi Finalist Vancouver Film Festival, Honorable Mention for Directing, and Best Romantic Drama Short.

It was a dream come true when her film screened at the famous Chinese Theater on Hollywood Blvd in Los Angeles, and she was presented with the Award of Best Romantic Drama Short. Most recently, Suzanne was awarded Best Actress in a Short/Film at the Silver State Film Festival (Roku Daily Shorts) 2020.

In the past few years, Suzanne has broadened her production skills by producing video documentaries for corporate companies, and most recently a cosmetic launch. These video docs are used on corporate websites. Additionally, she has partnered with many non-profit organizations such as Los Angeles Unified, LA's Best After-School Enrichment Program, and LAPD Gang Violence and Pregnancy Prevention Programs, teaching a Life Skills Program that she developed to mentor youth.

Suzanne teaches affordable online modeling classes to prospective models all over the United States. In Los Angeles, where she lives, she teaches online and private in-person classes. She also helps the models she works with produce their zed cards and find agent representation.

Stay in touch with Suzanne!

 SSchaack07@aol.com

 www.SuzanneVonSchaack.com

Made in the USA
Monee, IL
19 May 2021